End of tl
Propheteers

Exposing the Truth about Apocalyptic Predictions and the Blood Moon Scam

©2015 Lance Moore

Dedicated to Caroline Campbell Kaiser

With gratitude to my editor and encourager, Gaynor

Sky-Fy Publishing
Daphne, AL

All Rights Reserved

Table of Contents

Chapter One: *The End is Near… But I Have a Fat Retirement Plan*
Fear-Mongering for Fun and Profit

Chapter Two: *Jesus is Coming… Look Busy!*
Bad Theology Underlying the End Times View

Chapter Three: *I See a Bad Moon Rising*
The Problem with Blood Moons & Shemitah-dating

Chapter Four: *The Glass is Half Empty*
The Danger of Doomsday Pessimism

Chapter Five:
Rumors of Our Death Are Greatly Exaggerated
Failed Predictions of Hal Lindsey and Friends

Chapter Six: *Desperately Seeking Antichrist!*
666 Problems in Detecting the False Messiah

Chapter Seven:
Pot Calling Kettle, Pot Calling Kettle
False Prophets, False Profits, and True Hypocrisy

Chapter Eight: *Two Sides of the Same Coin*
Christian and Islamic Apocalypticism

Chapter Nine: *Deep and Wide*
A Deeper, More Thorough Study of Meaning

Chapter Ten: *Left Behind, or Right Ahead?*
Political Bias and the End Times Movement

Chapter Eleven: *Hope vs. Despair*
Is There a Future for the Church?

Chapter One: *The End is Near…*
But I Have a Fat Retirement Plan
Fear-Mongering for Fun and Profit

The disciples asked Jesus, "...when will this happen, and what will be the sign of your coming and of the end of the age?' Jesus answered: 'Watch out that no one deceives you."
~*Matthew 24:3-4*

"Then they gathered around him and asked him, 'Lord, are you at this time going to restore the kingdom to Israel?' He said to them: 'It is not for you to know the times or dates the Father has set by his own authority.'"
~*Jesus, in Acts 1:6-7*

Imagine this scenario: the Soviets reveal a new technology, a horrific weapon capable of, for example, reducing all of New York City to ash and bone. And the Soviets demonstrate this weapon in a remote location, so we know it is not a scare tactic. The "doomsday bomb" is real. Next imagine a mainstream minister, a man of impeccable integrity and respected gravitas, standing before a crowd and connecting the dots: the weapon and its time in history match the ancient prophecies of Holy Scripture. The Bible predicted this day would come, this *End of Days*, this Apocalypse Now.

"This is it… the sign of the Second Coming!" the preacher emphatically announces. People don't panic when they hear this, but they do see the dots connecting into a frame, the frame and canvas on which they begin to view all world events. Everything else changes in light of this new knowledge: their politics, their plans, hopes and worldview, and most of all, the tone of their religious expression.

The above scenario already happened. The time was 1949, and the man was a young Rev. Billy Graham, and the urgency was clear: the Russians detonated a plutonium bomb, code-named *First Lightning* —more powerful than what we had used to level Nagasaki and Hiroshima. The nuclear arms race had begun. Graphic descriptions of the nightmarish destruction our weapons had wrought upon Japan matched the fiery apocalypse predicted in Revelation, and Rev. Graham was quick to draw the comparison. Graham's sincere apocalyptic warning turned out to be a false alarm: the end did not come in the 1940's or 50's.

The Earth as the *Eveready* Bunny: *Still Going and Going*

The End also did not come in the early Sixties with the Cuban missile crisis. It did not come in the Seventies, despite Hal Lindsey's warnings, despite a *TIME* magazine cover that showed planet earth in the shape of a hand-grenade, with the admonition that time was running out. The end did not come in the 1980's despite the "Nuclear Doomsday Clock" ticking down to 11:59 and growing tensions with the USSR over its huge nuclear arsenal. Nor did the end come in 1988, despite a Bible expert /NASA engineer listing 88 reasons why Jesus would *absolutely positively* return in '88. Nor did it come in 1998, fifty years after the reformation of the nation Israel… an event that some Bible interpreters had pointed to as Jesus' meaning when he warned that "this generation," the one witnessing the rebirth of Israel, would also be the generation that would see his Second Coming (Mark 13:30). Scholars have never reached a consensus as to whether Jesus meant the generation listening to him *then*, the generation of the *time of the rebirth*, or just a *generic* reference to "this generation" as the human species? Whatever the case, the Second Coming obviously did not happen during that first generation of Christians, nor did it happen during the generation of those born in 1948 (because most scholars agree that a biblical "generation" is a span of either 40 years or 50 years).

Nor did the End come at the close of the second millennium, despite a thousand years of fear about that date, and then with news-media and computer programmers warning that an anomaly in IBM computers could cause a catastrophic computer failure as the clock struck midnight at 2000 AD. Nor did it happen with the onset of 2001 AD, the time the math nitpickers cited as the *true* start of the new millennium. Nor did it happen when the Twin Towers fell in New York, nor did it happen during the stock market Crash of 2007-2008, nor did things end, more recently, when bird flu and Ebola made us worry about pandemics.

Zombie Attack
Remember that zombie attack at JFK airport in New York a few years back? Just turned out to be Keith Richards and the Rolling Stones coming to town. (Sorry, couldn't resist stealing that joke.) And finally, despite many a warning on *YouTube* that President Barack Obama would be the charismatic, all-powerful antichrist who would usher in the New Age Tribulation, there is still no sign that any politician can muster more than a 39% approval rating these days. With catastrophes, holocaust, wars, earthquakes, famines, Blood Moons, all sorts of numerological and astronomical alignments… for 2,000 years, they've been warning us. But like the *Eveready* Bunny, the world keeps going and going.

Saint Paul thought the End of the Age would happen in his lifetime, before the end of the first century AD. Near the end of the First Millennium, much of the Western world feared that the year 1,000 AD (or 999 or 1001) would be the end of time. German historian Heinrich von Sybel wrote of this panic: "As the first thousand years of our calendar drew to an end, in every land of Europe the people expected with certainty the destruction of the world. Some squandered their substance in riotous living, others bestowed it for the salvation of their souls on churches and convents, bewailing multitudes lay by day and by night about the altars…." Sybel may have exaggerated the panic, but no doubt the concept was widespread in anticipation of the 999 AD "odometer rollover." And it was "*déjà vu* all over again" in 1999, with the "Y2K bug."

Nothing New Under the Sun

There is also nothing modern about the apocalypticism [see Chapter Two for definitions of topical "jargon terms"] we've seen in the last 20 years. It rests heavily on mathematical extrapolations of Jewish prophecy (2,500 years old), and on some odd ideas formed in the 1800's (200 years old). This latter includes two religious movements or schools of thought: **Millerism** and **Dispensationalism**. In 1833, Rev. William Miller published a detailed paper forecasting that the Second Advent of Jesus Christ would be in the year 1843 (the return of Christ being synonymous with the end of our world as we know it). Miller had spent years with his nose in Scripture and textbooks, particularly examining the symbolism in the prophecies of Daniel, to arrive at certainty that the end was near. By the end of 1844, with no sign of apocalypse, one Millerite wrote, "Our fondest hopes and expectations were blasted, and such a spirit of weeping came over us as I never experienced before.... We wept, and wept, till the day dawn."[1] Miller's failure did not stop John Darby from his similar Dispensationalist view of history, as both Darby and Cyrus Scofield tried to impose a Jewish time-clock to divide modern history into God-designed epochs (Dispensations). Among many warnings, Darby proclaimed the invention of the telegraph as a harbinger of Armageddon and a tool of the devil. Wow, he would have really hated the internet! The point is, with the latest best-sellers, from Blood Moons to secret Bible codes, there's really nothing new here. For two millennia, through a rehashing of old theories, the fear-mongering, self-proclaimed prophets have cried wolf... again and again. Some have been sincere, some have been shysters, but all have been...

**Dead Wrong
Every…
Single…
Time.**

Tomorrow Never Comes

First, a word to believers: I am not dismissing the supernatural. I am not a scoffer. I am not cynical by nature. I'm a Christian who believes God's prophets of old *have* foreseen future events. What I distrust are self-proclaimed modern prophets who make careless interpretations and crystal ball predictions that go well beyond the limits outlined in Scripture.

And, yes, I believe The End *could* come tomorrow. But I won't bet on it. I will not waste a moment worrying about an event that has been fruitlessly anticipated and falsely forecast for two thousand years. In fact, that's what Jesus literally commanded, "Do not worry about tomorrow." He also warned that no one knows the day or the hour…not the angels, not even the Son of God. And we opened this chapter with words from Jesus that should, alone, be enough to give End Times writers pause: **"It is not for you to know the times or dates the Father has set by his own authority."** (Acts 1:7) Considering the original Greek words used in this verse for "know" (*gnosis*) and "times and dates" (*chronos* and *kairos*), we can accurately paraphrase to conclude that Jesus was telling us to *quit trying to decipher the divine mysteries about the times and signs… that's God's business.*

But the Hal Lindseys and John Hagees of this world, in their arrogance, purport to have more inside knowledge than Jesus the Christ. The question is **not**, "Are any of these 'End-Timers' right about Jesus' return?" Jesus said plainly they *cannot* know, only the Father-God knows. So the question is, "Are the End Timers **arrogantly ignorant**, or **intentionally fraudulent**?"

Answer: at the very least, they are *exploitative*. To say the money they have reaped is substantial is an understatement. Has the phrase "obscene wealth" gone out of fashion? Thus I'm probably not the first person to coin an obvious term for those who have made a fortune from books on prophecy: ***propheteers***, from *prophet* and *profiteer* with a bit of *racketeer* and *buccaneer* thrown in. Pirates and racketeers indeed: the gross revenue from End of Time category books and tapes (counting fiction and non-fiction) is **well over a billion dollars!** Considering that Jesus Christ preached his most strident sermons against excessive wealth, we can use "gross revenue" with both definitions of "gross" when it comes to these "Christian" writers. Actually, buccaneers never had it as good as these propheteers: we are talking about *multiple mansions and private jets rich*. Tim Lahaye alone has made over $100 million dollars from End Time books/movies. He is not the only one who seems far more interested in Profits than Prophets.[2] And it is indeed a "racket," because it is all built upon a foundation of falsehood. (More about evangelists' greed in a later chapter.)

Religious "Porn"?

But what about the average reader who consumes this stuff? Is there anything wrong with having an interest in this subject, in buying books and watching movies about the End Times? It can be argued that it is a harmless diversion, no worse than any other leisure activity. And at least books such as *The Left Behind Series* are marketed as fiction… no harm in a bit of escapist fantasy, right?

On the other hand, some who become overly-obsessed with the topic may be guilty of a harmful indulgence not unlike porn addiction: obsession with scintillating words and images that are all flash and no substance. Okay, maybe that's too harsh of a comparison. At the least, End Times obsessions can take away from time spent on more meaningful Bible study.

Some who delve deep into the End Times pool find it titillating to believe one is among an elite *cognoscenti*, a cult of super-believers who are "in the know" about a deep mystery. There's a sense of empowerment that comes from lording it over the pagans, in effect saying: "Ah, you poor deluded lemmings… you don't know the REAL Jesus, nor do you know the REAL prophecies that are unfolding under your nose." In their eschatological view, they are the Christians who will "get the last laugh." After all, there is nothing funnier than seeing your enemies—the infidels, the unbelievers—staring in amazement as you ecstatically float up into the air (**butt naked**, according to the version by Tim LaHaye and Jerry Jenkins) toward heaven whilst they are left writhing in the flames of a nuclear conflagration. As Larry the Cable Guy might put it, "That's funny right thar… I don't care who ya are!" One can't read the "Left Behind" series without sensing that some Christians are all too happy to be God's chosen-elite "Tribulation Force" that watches the world burn around them.

It's such wicked fun to be the elite ones "in the club." When I was a first-grader, my brothers and I were invited to join a neighbor kid's club… his parents had indulged him with a small playhouse in the backyard. Another neighbor boy would come by while we were inside the little clubhouse with the door locked, begging us to let him come in and join. My friends taunted the boy, insulting him for no reason other than he was the odd man out. Over a few weeks it became something of a game. He'd come by and throw rocks at the door and we'd open a shutter and throw something back and tell him to go away. Then one day my buddies informed me that the stranger boy had moved away and would no longer be assailing our club house. I said in childish disappointment, "Dang, now we'll have to find a new enemy!" What I stated at six-years-old is a sick, selfish mindset that, thankfully, did not follow me into more mature years. I now see the satanic nature of taking pleasure at being part of the "in group." Such *us vs. them* exclusiveness is not truly Christian. The lifestyle taught by Jesus is based on the broadest possible answer to the question, "Who is my neighbor?" (See the story of the Good Samaritan.) The exclusionary view of End Time propheteers and the joy they seem to feel at being victors in the bloodbath is only one of my criticisms, but perhaps the most troubling.

The Boy Who Cried Wolf: A Loss of Credibility

The most harmful sin of the Hal Lindseys of this world is they cause a loss of credibility for Christianity. When Christian leaders claim divine insight into the "secret messages" in Scripture, emphatically predicting specific dates for specific events (wrongly), it destroys the credibility of those leaders. For some people, it erodes the authority of the Bible itself. In commenting on the latest "Blood Moon" prophecies, David James of "The Alliance for Biblical Integrity," wrote: "This mishandling of the perfect Word of God, by those who should know better, is a blight on the precious Body of Christ."

It is even worse than the "boy who cried wolf." In the fable, a boy, for the fun of inciting panic in the crowd, falsely cried wolf once (and no wolf came) and then twice (and no wolf came). But the third time he cried out, now to deaf ears, an actual wolf came. For those who forget the moral of the story, the boy saw how truly dangerous it is to squander one's credibility.

Alarmist authors like Hal Lindsey, Tim LaHaye, and John Hagee not only have exponentially exceeded the "boy who cried wolf" in the number of false alarms, but they have yet to have ANY wolf come! Certainly, they could point to events in history and find some biblical prophecy that might loosely match it. But the same sleight of hand has been done with the pagan prophecies of Nostradamus—using his vague poetry to project synchronicities onto world events is all too easy. But for the End Times bunch, none of the major outcomes they have predicted have arrived in our times… no worldwide famine, no World War Three, no California falling into the ocean, no worldwide darkness, no single antichrist world leader.

Another major problem among End Time authors is their tendency to employ a **constricted, literalistic view of Scripture**. Almost by necessity (to sustain their specific predictions), they reduce Scripture to the Lowest Common Denominator. Most Bible passages have double or triple meanings. The Bible is full and rippling with metaphors, historical context, poetic allusions, and multi-dimensional subtleties that they sandpaper flat, so that today's headlines can be decoupaged on top of an unwrinkled Holy Writ. This is a "double-problem." First, it misleads/misinforms people on the subject of End Times, and second, it pulls people into a false theology and a poor Bible study method that then carries over into their broader theological understanding (or lack of it). We will examine this more closely in the next chapter.

~~~

Chapter Two: *Jesus is Coming ... Look Busy!*
Bad Theology Underlying the End Times View

"For sin shall no longer be your master, because you are not under the law, but under grace."
~*Romans 6:14*

"See to it that no one takes you captive through hollow and deceptive philosophy, which depends on human tradition and the elemental spiritual forces of this world rather than on Christ."
~*Colossians 2:8*

My critics may accuse me of an *ad hominem* attack for my use of the term *propheteers*. So be it. Misleading people and making a fortune by fearmongering warrants a harsh label. I am not attacking everyone in the field of prophecy. We would be mistaken to think all the scores of writers, pastors and leaders in the End Times movement are/were just money-making shysters. Some firmly believed their predictions. They're often college- educated, sincere Christians who invested enormous hours reading and researching the topic. Nevertheless, if they are wrong, should their error not be exposed? Does not Scripture order us to "expose" "fruitless deeds" (Ephesians 5:11)? Saint Paul instructs pastors to "...correct, rebuke and encourage..." (2 Timothy 4:2). As an ordained Methodist minister, I am fulfilling that directive by writing this.

The question remains, regardless of the End Time writers' motives, **how can they be so consistently and utterly wrong?** Besides what should have been an obvious warning from Jesus himself ("No man can know the day or the hour...."), it is now clear that their *method* of Bible interpretation is **broken at its core**.

Most End Time propheteers put a controlling "spin" on Scripture using discredited Bible-study methods such as

Dispensationalism, excessive literalism, and proof-texting (terms that will be explained shortly). The very nature of their approach to Scripture runs counter to good theology. I define good theology as that which fosters a deeper understanding of a Loving God rooted in a scholarly and contextual reverence for Holy Scripture with the aim of bringing all people to encounter the love and grace of Christ. Instead...

End Time theories almost always:
•begin with the approach that a wrathful God will inflict horrible suffering and death upon millions of human beings.
•emphasize a works-righteousness notion that we must change our behavior and "do right" lest we suffer a horrible, painful death.
•distract us from living *in the now*… they put too much focus on what may or may not happen a year from now.
•feed a pessimistic, fatalistic view of human nature and human history. If God so controls every country, every politician, in such a micro-managed way that events are forced to happen exactly on specific dates, that rules out human free will.
•use a selective, out-of-context Bible "study" method known as "proof-texting" that cherry-picks verses favorable to their argument while ignoring contrary verses.
•major in the minor—they carefully count the leaves on trees but offer no way to guide us through the forest. Ultimately, they do not offer us any advice about what to do with their claim that the world is ending, other than a vague, unspecified, "Get ready."
•presume an Old Testament, legalistic/punitive view of religion rather than a New Testament forgiving, redemptive approach. They call us back to Judaism, putting too much emphasis on Jewish rituals, holy days and festivals. This ignores much of the teaching of Jesus and Paul, who set us

free from the ritualistic obligations of Judaism in favor of a Christian faith rooted in love and grace. At their worst, End Time entrepreneurs are greedy peddlers of the "Galatian heresy," long ago rejected by Orthodox Christendom.

Definitions and Disclaimers

Let me pause for an aside: for clarity, some definitions:
-eschatology: the religious study of "end things." Rooted in the idea that God plans and works through history, sets epochs or eras for certain things to happen in human affairs, all building toward a climax of suffering (*Tribulation*), divine judgment/destruction, then renewal (Heaven/Paradise reborn).
-End Times, End of Days, End of the World: in religious terms, these phrases refer to the destruction of the current civilization, the obliteration of human governments, and a re-setting of the cosmic clock... all to make way for a New World (and/or Heaven) and the future New Age of God. In this book, I use "End Times writers" to refer to a particular type of date-setting, sensationalizing Christian writers and their popular, exploitative books.
-apocalypse and apocalypticism: literally means "a revelation of something hidden," as in an uncovering of the secrets of the end of the world; applied to a variety of religious End Times scenarios.
-Rapture and Tribulation: not present in all End Times theories, but Rapture refers to God snatching (Latin *raptus*) Christians out of this decaying world, immediately before, during or after the Tribulation. Most pop writers hope the Rapture will save Christians from the pain of the Tribulation, a short period of worldwide suffering from horrible plagues and a final, bloody holy war called *Armageddon*.
-Armageddon: the ultimate battle between good and evil, usually expected to take place near Israel. The word Apocalypse is sometimes used synonymously for

Armageddon, but that is not technically correct. The Francis Ford Coppola war movie, *Apocalypse Now*, should actually have been called *Armageddon Now*.

-messiah: a term used by several world religions, including Judaism, Christianity, and Islam, that refers to a god-like human savior. In Hebrew, he is the "anointed one," the prophesied One ordained by God as a divine king. Often viewed as a political leader and even a conquering warrior, the messiah is seen as a liberator and redeemer of individuals and society... but he may also bring Armageddon and judgment.

-antichrist: Satan's counterfeit and counterbalancing copy of the messiah, usually thought to be a Hitler-like evil dictator [I choose to not capitalize "antichrist," because I will not show the character that much respect, and the Bible did not capitalize the word as a proper name or title, either.]

-Second Coming: for Christians, Jesus is the Messiah who has already come to earth but will come again, and His "second coming" is associated with the End Times.

Now a disclaimer: This book is **not** intended as a scholarly or comprehensive review of the history of eschatology. Plenty of books already exist of that nature. My book is intended for the average reader as a persuasive rebuttal of writers who claim to know the secrets of End Times. Nothing else.

Listen to Jesus and Paul

Back to our chapter's topic: bad theology among End Times writers. Most Christian writers with a "world will end tomorrow" mindset ignore two very important directives from Jesus and Paul:

1. End-Timers are rejecting Jesus' command that we not worry about tomorrow and *not* make physical preparations for the End Time. Matthew 24:17-18: "Let no one on the housetop go down to take anything out of the house. Let no one in the field go back to get their cloak." Many "prophecy" websites that tell us to "get ready" also promote "survivalist" gear/food for sale. This is not a Christian response, even if one believed "the signs of the end" were here. When the days of Tribulation come, Jesus says in Matthew 24, we should not be obsessed with stockpiling supplies in our basements (a paraphrase of "Let no one... go back to get their cloak."). No, the only preparation Jesus asks us to do (see Matthew 25:31-46), if the end seems to be approaching, is the same thing Christians should *always* be doing: feeding the hungry, visiting the sick and the outcast, caring for "the least of these."

2. End-Timers reject Paul's teaching that Christianity should be "post-Jewish," available not just to those who observe Jewish traditions but to Gentiles (non-Jews, "pagans"). Many End-Timers have an obsession with the legalistic rituals and rules of Judaism, in sharp contrast to what Jesus and Paul both emphasized. They are what Paul called "Judaizers."

Note: An apology to my Jewish friends. My wife fears this section comes off as anti-Semitic, which is not my intention. The debate at hand is by a Christian (myself) addressing Christians (that is, the End Time writers), and it requires that we consider the question of whether or not their theological understanding of prophecy is consistent with orthodox Christianity. The propheteers, generally speaking, have a very strict, conservative view of our faith, so it is fair to measure their self-consistency. Put another way: the measure of harsh judgment they apply to people who fall outside of their narrow orthodoxy is a measure I'm reflecting back upon them by asking, "Are they truly consistently Christian, or are they reverting to the very Judaism they otherwise believe Jesus has transformed into Christianity?"

New Jews

The late Herbert W. Armstrong taught his cult-like "Worldwide Church of God" to become modern day Jews, expending their energies following Jewish dietary customs, rituals and holidays/festivals. To the contrary, Paul in Colossians 2:16-17 asserted: "Do not let anyone judge you by what you eat or drink, or with regard to a religious festival, a New Moon celebration or a Sabbath day. These are a shadow of the things that were to come; the reality, however, is found in Christ." For 2,000 years, the most devout mainstream Christians and the best biblical scholars have unanimously agreed that Jesus, Peter and Paul moved us past Jewish restrictions and a "works-righteousness" legalism to a new freedom in Christ, a salvation given by grace, not earned by deeds. If you remove the Jewish history and theology lessons re-spun by Hagee, Lindsey and Jonathan Cahn, there would be very little left in their books! Most of their "predictions" depend upon using a Jewish system of dates as a lens for current events, and an unbiblical assumption that America is now God's chosen nation. As a Christian, I do not see much New Testament support for those formulas. (Yes, the Book of Revelation uses Jewish symbolism as a metaphor, but John's vision is not a literal blueprint for future events... it is a Christian allegory not a Jewish extrapolation.) They ignore Jesus' warning that you can't put new wine (Christianity) into old wine skins (Judaism). This is not "anti-semitic" —Jesus was a Jew. I appreciate and honor Jewish tradition and history, and every Christian should study it as the context for the life and teachings of Christ and the early Church. But orthodox Christianity is **post**-Jewish... we cannot go backward.

Just as Hagee bases his End Time theory on Jewish-dated "blood moons," similarly, Jonathan Cahn's *The Mystery of the Shemitah* hangs on the Jewish observance of seven-year cycles.[3] Every seven-year cycle, he says, culminates in a

Sabbatical year known as a "Shemitah" in transliterated Hebrew. Rooted in sevens, Cahn begins his process of looking for predictive patterns with the year of the destruction of the second Temple. Of course, even that date is uncertain, as scholars date it variously anywhere from 68 to 70 AD (CE) in the secular calendar. But by counting sevens from that event, Cahn calculates that the next (from the time he wrote) Shemitah year ends September 13, 2015... at which point, he predicts, a "catastrophic" disaster will befall America. This does not leave much time for Cahn to spend the profits from his #1 best-selling book!

Speaking for God?

Cahn's "Shemitah" theory will be examined further in a later chapter. But for now, one more point on the topic of a Judaized, works-righteousness Christianity: Cahn apparently speaks for God the Judge when he says: "If America ever turned away from God, then the same judgments that fell upon ancient Israel would fall upon America." Does Cahn think Jesus died on the cross for nothing? Has he not read Galatians 3:13-14?: "Christ redeemed us from the curse of the law by becoming a curse for us... [via the crucifixion]. He redeemed us in order that the blessing given to Abraham might come to the Gentiles through Christ Jesus." America is **not** a New Jerusalem; we are a land mostly of Gentiles, under the blessing of the New Testament, not under a curse from the Old. Disregarding the New Covenant is, as Hebrews 6:6 says, like "they are crucifying the Son of God all over again."

I'm sure the propheteers will throw other verses at me to bolster their works-righteousness case, but I submit that these verses from Paul and Jesus trump whatever card they may play: "Therefore, there is now no condemnation for those who are in Christ Jesus, because through Christ Jesus the law of the Spirit who gives life has set you free from the law of sin and death." (Romans 8:1-2) "For God did not send his

Son into the world to condemn the world, but to save the world through him." (John 3:17) You can quote to me the fact that Jesus said of the Old Testament, "Do not think that I have come to abolish the Law or the Prophets; I have not come to abolish them but to fulfill them." (see Matthew 5:17-18) But in the very same passage, in Matthew 5:38-39, Jesus blatantly overturned the Old Testament Law of Leviticus regarding an "Eye for an eye, and a tooth for tooth...." Jesus **completely reversed** this Law, changing retribution into "turn the other cheek." Thus, clearly, His definition of "fulfilling" the Law means to radically re-interpret it on the side of peace and grace.

The Arrogance of End Times Assertiveness

Most of the propheteers have two other flaws in common: one, their indefatigable self-confidence, and two, a presumptuous, literal view of Scripture that puts entirely too much weight on the parsing of words in each discrete verse, rather than taking a broad, contextual, metaphorical view of Scripture. I've already mentioned their tendency toward *proof-texting*, but what's more, within each selective "proof-text" verse, they burden every phrase and noun with exclusive, specific meanings when, in fact, **most biblical words, and verses, have several possible meanings**. This is one reason why there are so many translations/versions of the English Bible: two of the best Greek scholars, honorable men guided by the Holy Spirit, will each come up with slightly different English translations. But the End Timers act as if they have a monopoly on truth, imposing their finite and subjective definitions, claiming they know the "objective" truth. God's divine Truth is objective, but language cannot help but be *subjective*. Every human has a unique life experience that filters the way we understand language. And every single word in Greek or Hebrew—just like each word in English—has at least two or more possible meanings! Put together into phrases and sentences, each verse also has multiple possibilities: it may be a figure of speech, or an allusion to Hebrew tradition, or in rare spots, include a symbol or code... even puns and jokes are found in Scripture. Since the propheteers have a pre-set agenda, they choose the word-meaning that fits their singular prejudices, and then build upon it, like kids building an elaborate treehouse only to find that the trunk of the tree is rotten.

Another Reply to My Critics

Let me insert here a pre-emptive answer to those who may, fairly enough, criticize me by pointing out that I am equally guilty of proof-texting. I do indeed use selective Bible quotes to make my case herein. The difference is that I am not the one making extraordinary claims. The Scriptures I select are to point out the very verses that the End Time writers ignored or glossed over. I am not building a systematic case purporting to prove prophecies from 2,000 to 4,000 years ago apply to this exact moment in time. **They are.** Thus, the burden is on them. We are testing their claim, and examining their failure to see Scripture comprehensively—and that requires that we point out the specific verses they have overlooked, verses which contradict their thesis.

Your Faith Can Beat Up My Faith

The fallacy of Bible inerrancy and literalism is not confined to "End Times Prophecy," but it is in this field that we can demonstrate the utter failure of such an approach to religion. The literalists fail to accept that the Bible can be *true* in a telescopic view without being very *precise* in a microscopic view. They refuse to admit that, while God's Word is true, and reflects the perfection of God, it comes to us **through imperfect human language.** Yes, I'm being redundant—but the point bears repeating. Human language in our fallen world can only be flawed and finite. As the Bee

Gees' song puts it, "It's only words, and words are all I have...." Using words to describe the divine and the infinite is like asking a monkey to sketch a Rembrandt with a pencil. It's a human process. The only way to come to a closer understanding of truth, using the broken clay vessel of human words, is to look at the big picture—the context and culture—in which we find those words.

Fundamentalists act like bullies, not just disagreeing with other views, but labeling variant voices as *unfaithful* or even *evil*. They tend to think there is a moral superiority in holding to moral absolutes, dismissing the use of cultural and contextual studies as "subjective moral relativism." I do indeed believe there are moral absolutes that God has put in place in the universe (starting with the Law of Gravity, for example). But some conservatives fail to admit that their understanding, interpretation and application of those "moral absolutes" is itself a subjective assessment. Our very understanding of language is based on preconceived notions that are a product of where and when we were raised, which books we've studied, which experiences we've had. It takes great arrogance to assert that "MY experience and knowledge is the Absolute, because I am morally superior." They don't actually say those words, but their dismissive attitude toward "Liberals" and "Intellectuals" does, in effect, reflect an attitude that their faith is stronger than mine, and their view of Scripture is "right" because they have a closer relationship with the Holy Spirit.

Bad with Math

From all that I have studied (and I have studied the Bible all of my life), Scripture was never intended to be a precise schematic or mathematical formula. The New Testament story, in particular, is not intended as a weather report or court stenographer's verbatim. Take Scripture in *gestalt*, not sliced and diced by a Ronco Vegematic. God's word is more about the quantum landscape spread across the eons than about the movements of a molecule in these five seconds. "But," you may argue, "Jesus said God counts the very hairs of our heads." Yes, God does... but He* [I choose not use inclusive language for God for simplicity's sake] saw no reason to give the exact count in Scripture! In fact, almost each and every occasion where a specific numeral is given in Scripture (e.g. 7, 12, 40, 70, 153, 666), the numeral represents a bigger concept or symbol, and was not intended to be numbers and decimals in an accountant's ledger. Applying mathematics and dating to the Bible is an exercise in futility... and history has proven that. As with almost every failed End Time prediction, the false prophets and opportunists try to squeeze all they can out of a "significant date," even when it means re-jiggering the timing after it once proves false! Edgar C. Whisenant (more on him later) did this with his confident math-based prediction of Jesus returning in 1988.

When Whisenhant was proven wrong in 1988, he "re-calculated" several times (and sold more brochures in the process) for several successive years before giving up. The same math/dating error has already begun to happen regarding the "blood moons theory." The website "Watch For the Day" stated in 2008 that the "Blood Moons" theory "would place the Tribulation as beginning sometime at the close of 2008—this year."[4] Well, things haven't been a picnic for me the last 7 years, but I wouldn't call it a Tribulation! The same website stated that there are "three possible Rapture days, which is the Feast of Trumpets 2008, 2009, and 2010." Those days came and went without event... another failed prophecy, and yet another example of the failure of literalistic, narrow-view proof-texting.

This is one reason I feel compelled to write this book: my hope is that the keen interest many people have on the topic might be turned for the good. Good theology and good Bible scholarship are not abstract trivia. Coming to a better understanding of the deep riches of what God is trying to say to us could enrich our individual spiritual lives and make for a better society. **When we hear of "wars and rumors of wars," it would be good if we turned to the Bible's teachings on peace and human reconciliation, rather than dismissing world events as just concrete steps to an inevitable apocalypse.** Jesus said that even when we hear those rumors, "the end is still to come." The message of Revelation is NOT "horrible wars are coming, so just hunker down and hide." No, the message is that ultimately Jesus will be victorious, and regardless of when that will be, we are called to be loving and peaceful Christians who take care of "the least of these" until then.

The Glee Club

In contrast, some writers of End Times scenarios seem to take glee at the prospect of gruesome misery and massacre of millions of human lives. Author Tim LaHaye tells of how he came up with the idea for his "Left Behind" series: "This is an idea that the Lord gave me when I was on a plane. The airline captain came out of his cave and he started flirting with the head stewardess. I noticed that he had a wedding ring on. She did not. I began to see the sparks flying between these two and as he went back into the [cockpit], I got to thinking, *What if the Rapture occurred right now? On this plane, a third of these people would be gone. It would be pandemonium.* I imagined this guy, married to I assumed, a Christian, and all of the sudden it would dawn on him, "When I get home, my wife will be gone, and I have been left behind."" (quoted in *Vanity Fair* magazine, December 2005)

This gives us a window into how Tim LaHaye thinks: observing the behavior of two people he knows nothing about, he thinks the worst. He judges what could be old friends sharing a joke to instead be a lusty, sexual flirtation, behavior so un-Christian that both are deserving of being "left behind" by Jesus, in LaHaye's theology. But for all he knew, the stewardess might have left her wedding ring home soaking in jewelry cleaner, and might have been *married* to the pilot!

If I were to apply an "eye for an eye" and utilize the same kind of **rash judgment,** I could say this of LaHaye: we can almost taste the envy LaHaye had toward the pilot—the successful man-in-uniform who is also having "success" (in LaHaye's mind) flirting with an attractive stewardess. Then it is not far-fetched to read between the lines and find the consoling satisfaction that LaHaye felt when he envisioned that pilot being excluded from the Rapture... abandoned by his "Christian" wife and doomed to a fiery death, apparently for the sin of flirting while married.

Again, this reveling in judgment and punishment is not consistent with what Jesus taught. God's words of grace include Luke 6:37, "Do not judge, and you will not be judged. Do not condemn, and you will not be condemned." and Romans 3:23-24: "For all have sinned and fall short of the glory of God, and all are justified freely by his grace through the redemption that came by Christ Jesus."

The Predestination Problem

Yet another theological problem with the prophecy movement is how quickly they are willing to deny our free will. If God micromanages the cosmos and pre-ordains (pre-plans and presets) events to happen, what point is there in our living? If we have no choice in the matter, if we are mere puppets manipulated by God's string-pulling, then why not just throw our hands up and say, "Nothing we do, say or choose matters... because God is manipulating it all!" For example, explaining the title of his End Times book, Jonathan Cahn writes: "*The Harbinger* is the revealing of an ancient mystery that holds the secret of what has happened and is happening... in modern times... [and God] ordains the words uttered by world leaders, who have no idea what they're saying—so precise that times and dates given more than three thousand years ago set the time and dates on which some of the most monumental events of recent times take place."

So, if world leaders are merely God's mouthpieces—if they are mere robots programmed by God-the-master-computer-programmer—then humanity is not free. Moreover, how could a just and fair God then condemn such "evil" men to Hell, if God Himself is the one putting words in their mouths and causing events to happen to fit His time schedule? Cahn and his like-minded fellow authors write assertions like this without any deep thought about the ramifications. Their theology is irrational and inconsistent. They paint a God to fit their scenario, and when the picture gets too big, they just "crop" God's portrait to fit their limited frame.

If you study the lives and writings of the best theologians across the centuries, you will find few of them expending much thought and energy about Rapture, Tribulation, or Armageddon. The great theologians are concerned with how we can better know God in Christ, how we can receive and respond to God's message of love and grace, both collectively as a Church and individually as "agents of reconciliation." I realize that I also sound judgmental in assessing the Apocalyptic genre´, but there is a thin line between discernment vs. condemnation. I am not condemning the propheteers to Hell, but I am, humbly as I can by being rooted in Scripture, questioning their logic and hopefully widening their view of what God would have us focus upon in this new millennium.

~~~

Chapter Three: *I See a Bad Moon Rising*
(with Apologies to Creedence Clearwater Revival)
The Problem with Blood Moons (& Shemitah-dating)

Jesus replied: "Watch out that you are not deceived. For many will come in my name, claiming...'The time is near.' Do not follow them."
  ~Luke 21:8

"Have nothing to do with godless myths and old wives' tales; rather, train yourself to be godly."
  ~1st Timothy 4:7

Where do we start in addressing the multiple problems with "End Time" theories? The latest theory of the "Blood Moons" is in the news and may be of first interest to many readers, though in the long history of failed predictions and false hype, there is nothing particularly new or compelling about it. Indeed, in this field, there is "nothing new under the sun" ...not even the moon.

But what are the "Four Blood Moons," "Tetrads" and "Shemitah Year" all about? End Time writers/speakers such as Mark Biltz, John Hagee and Jonathan Cahn assert that significant events in contemporary history echo events in Jewish history, all transpiring around either the calendar of Jewish holy festivals, or connected with astrological movements, especially lunar eclipses that appear in clumps such as the four "Blood Moon tetrads" within an 18 month span. That was a long sentence, but don't blame me, I'm not the one who comes up with these theories!

Nonsense and Non-science
  In his book, *Four Blood Moons*, Hagee is quick to cite scientists to bolster his authority in order to drum up fear, such as references to NASA, and a quote from physicist Michio Kaku about solar flares. But whenever science

disputes his theory, Hagee is happy to just ignore the facts of science. For example, to speak of stars "falling" to earth—part of the Scripture (Joel 2) he uses for his Blood Moon theory— makes an astronomer laugh. And I'm not laughing at the *Scripture*, because I interpret that Scripture metaphorically. The mockery applies to Hagee's attempt to misapply a poetic meaning as if it were a literal science lesson. Another example: Hagee's reference to Joshua 10:12, where the "sun stood still." Hagee states that "God took total control of the sun" (to extend the length of the day for battle), but he fails to mention that science has long known the movement of the sun has nothing to do with the length of a day… it is the *earth's* rotation, not solar movement, that makes day and night. Knowing that fact, one has to either say the Bible was wrong in stating that God stopped the sun from moving, or else admit that Joshua is speaking metaphorically. Hagee asserts that anyone who does not take the Bible literally is a false prophet. So he has painted himself into a corner.

    Nevertheless, Pastor Hagee moves on undaunted. He continues to appeal to scientific authority and accuracy in his description of impending disaster… but his literalism fails again when he tries, in his book *Blood Moons,* to connect the "blood red" moon described in Scripture with real-life lunar eclipses. The color of the moon in a lunar eclipse ranges from pink to orange-red; the color of spilt blood is a rich crimson to maroon. And of course, the moon in an eclipse has not actually changed color from its normal shade of white and grey—the coloring is an effect of the atmosphere. It would be more "literal" to speak of a *reddish atmosphere* than of a blood moon. Professional astronomers (i.e. real scientists) do not regularly use the phrase "blood moon" or "blood moon tetrad" (well, they didn't until these books popularized the term). Hagee and Biltz assert that the Blood Moon tetrad of 2014 and 2015 will herald significant events related to biblical prophecy, citing verses to claim that these eclipses are fulfilling the sun, moon, and star signs in the Bible.

It's Not the End of the World

I hate to spoil the ending for you, but the final fourth Blood Moon of September 28th, 2015 will almost assuredly NOT be the end of the world. Mark Biltz tried to assert that the first blood moon (in this most recent tetrad series) marked "the Russian invasion of the Ukraine… the advance of Isis… the Ebola plague, upheaval in the Middle East, and economic meltdowns…."[5] Let's examine those claims:

•Invasion of Ukraine: tensions between Moscow and the Ukraine long preceded any "warning" by the 2014-2015 blood moon tetrad, and though Ukrainians hate the Russian threats, there has not been any full-scale invasion.

•Advance of Isis: also preceded any blood moon warning, and at this point, Isis is contained if not retreating.

•Ebola epidemic: Not to minimize the human pain in Africa, but in the U.S. and Israel (the only countries the propheteers seem concerned about), the impact of ebola is near zero.

•Middle East upheaval: as always, this is the easiest prediction to make. One could have predicted trouble in the Middle East and been correct in every decade of human existence… sadly, one can expect violence on *any* given day somewhere in the Middle East.

•Economic meltdown: so far during this tetrad, we've had nothing but improvement in the economy, and a record-high stock market. However, I would not be surprised if there is a market crash or calamity in the near future… not because of blood moons, but because of the simple rule, "What goes up must come down." The market is high now, inflated by borrowed money and artificially-low interest rates. But don't call me a prophet if there's a steep stock market decline this year… it just seems obvious. Markets always fluctuate.

Perhaps the best re-assurance that nothing horrible will

happen on the ultimate blood moon of September 28th, 2015, is the fact that John Hagee is advertising nothing but a fun day on his own JHM.org website. Even while Hagee's book spells doom for late September, his church calendar plans a fun, game-filled day just a few weeks later! His Cornerstone Church has planned for October 23-25, 2015, "a special time of celebration with Fun, Food, Fellowship, midway full of Games and FREE RIDES!" "Guest Speaker" (yes, at his own church) is to be a non-raptured Rev. Hagee. His church's website also has big events planned for Christmas… that's three months *after* the terrible events forecast for September, which he has called "the final curtain call before the Great Tribulation." Looks like the end of the world isn't such a bummer after all.

2 +2 = 5, That's the Accuracy of Biltz Math

So why have people taken Hagee and Biltz seriously? It is because, using "holy God-talk," they play a good game of matching big events with astronomical signs of the past. They try to connect the four lunar eclipses of 1493-1494 with a significant event in Jewish history, namely the Spanish Inquisition that included the expulsion of Jews who refused to convert to Catholicism… but the Spanish Inquisition began years before (in 1478). Even the specific royal proclamation cited by Biltz happened a year BEFORE the lunar eclipse. If God had been trying to send a predictive sign, His timing was way too late; the persecutions had been underway for years! It would be the equivalent of Wise Men seeing a star-sign, following it to Bethlehem, but arriving over a year AFTER Jesus was born, after his family returned to Nazareth… and all they found was a sign saying, "Jesus slept here!"

The Spanish Inquisition affected a relatively small number of Jews. By contrast, the Nazi Holocaust killed six million Jews… and there is no "blood moon tetrad" associated with it. Oops, guess God forgot to warn His Chosen People of that one! The only event of similar "Jewish significance" (to the Holocaust) that might be associated with blood moon tetrads is the reformation of the nation Israel on May 14th, 1948. But again, the nearest tetrad period is a year off: it was April 13th, 1949 through September 25th, 1950. Biltz seems to enjoy engaging fuzzy math.

Add to all these sloppy correlations the fact that two of the six "tetrad blood moon" events have *zero* connection to any significant event in Jewish history—and Hagee and Biltz even admit this.

Another tetrad they cite is Israel's dramatic victory in the Six Day War of June 5-10, 1967. Though Hagee and Biltz wish to claim this as a connection, the last eclipse of that tetrad—October 6, 1968—was well over a year after the war ended.

It is not surprising in the least that a newsworthy event in Israel and the Middle East will occur during a lunar eclipse… Israel is in the world news almost weekly! Biltz cites a Hamas rocket attack on April 16th as having been predicted by the blood moon of the next day. But the truth is, rockets attack Israel almost every week of the year! See the long list of rocket attacks in the link following, and you will see that this correlation is meaningless:
www://en.wikipedia.org/wiki/List_of_Palestinian_rocket_attacks_on_Israel,_2014

How Rare is a "Blood Tetrad"?

A lunar tetrad is four total lunar eclipses within about 18 months. The so-called tetrad is more common in some centuries than in others. In this twenty-first century, there will be a total of eight tetrads, while in the 17th, 18th and 19th centuries, there were none. So in those years we might call it rare, but for the twentieth and twenty-first centuries, they are not nearly as "rare" an astronomical event as Haley's

29

Comet. From the first century AD through the 21st century, the total will be 62 tetrads. The most recent two were in 2003-2004 and 2014-2015, with another tetrad coming in about 15 years. So tetrads are neither common nor particularly rare… they are just normally-recurring astronomical events.

Scriptural Problems with the Blood Moon Theory

The April 2014 and April 2015 total lunar eclipses do align with the feast of Passover, and the October 2014 and September 2015 total lunar eclipses align with the Feast of Tabernacles. This is not particularly remarkable. First of all, these feasts cover several days, and second, the Jewish calendar is a lunar calendar. So in any given year, it's not odd at all that a full moon could fall on or near the feasts of Passover (15 Nissan) and Tabernacles (15 Tishri). Statistically-speaking, it is not particularly significant for some Jewish festivals to be synchronous with a blood moon. It is no more an "amazing coincidence" than the fact that Christmas always lands near the winter solstice.

Moreover, one would think that if these were signs in the sky from God, they would be visible in Israel, especially in Hagee's Jewish- centered scenario. Israel is where the prophecies were originally given and where, according to all End Times authors, the prophetic events are to unfold. But of the four eclipses in 2014-2015, *only* the last one of the four could be seen from Israel —and barely visible for a short while before sunrise. This does not match the dramatic events prophesied in Joel, Revelation, and Matthew, which will be seen by every eye on earth and will include additional signs.

There is, in fact, nothing in the Bible that directly connects a "blood moon" with a lunar eclipse. In almost every case where it refers to the moon, the Scripture is speaking about figurative "dark days," a poetic image not much different than the Carpenters singing, "Rainy Days and Mondays always get me down." When the Scriptures warn of a bad time approaching by using the poetic language of darkness and shadows, it is not a weather report.

Another verse often cited on the matter is Matthew 24:29, where Jesus spoke of a future event in which "the sun will be darkened, and the moon will not give its light, and the stars will fall from heaven, and the powers of the heavens will be shaken." In a lunar eclipse, the stars do not dim nor fall. In Isaiah 13:10 the prophet also predicted bad days: "For the stars of the heavens and their constellations will not give their light; the sun will be dark at its rising and the moon will not shed its light." And again, that is not describing a lunar eclipse. Isaiah was predicting the overthrow of Babylon by the Assyrians, which occurred in 689 BC. Even the conservative, dispensationalist *Bible Knowledge Commentary* identifies this passage as containing "figures of speech suggesting all-encompassing destruction." In other words, it is something far bigger and more cataclysmic than a mere eclipse.

Hagee and Biltz hang much of their theory on Joel 2:31: "The sun will be turned to darkness and the moon to blood before the coming of the great and dreadful day of the Lord." The greater context of that Scripture includes an earthquake (verse 2:10). Earthquakes are not geologically related to lunar eclipses. Eclipses have no effect upon seismic activity. No major earthquake is connected with the key tetrads named by Hagee (1493, 1949, 1967).

Moot Moon Point

More damning to Hagee's theory regarding this passage is that other parts of the Bible show that the second chapter of Joel has **already occurred**. I am not the first to point out the second chapter of Acts clearly states that the prophecy of Joel 2 has already been fulfilled, making the whole "blood moon" theory a moot point. Just after Jesus had ascended to heaven,

God poured out the Holy Spirit on the early Christians to christen the Church (the "Day of Pentecost"). Saint Peter explained that THIS event was the fulfillment of Joel's prophecy. In Acts 2:16, Peter stated, "No, this is what was spoken of by the prophet Joel…" whereupon Peter quoted Joel 2:17-31. Hagee and Biltz say they treasure every single word of the Bible, yet they completely disregard Peter's words... because it destroys the foundation of their theories.

When Stretching Truth is Sketching Lies

Hagee is guilty of the same two central "sins" committed by most End Times authors: proof-texting Scripture (cherry-picking verses out of context), and exaggerating events and connections to prove their point. A few examples:
•In Hagee's *Four Blood Moons* book, he wrote: "The Bible and America's best scientists are in agreement that planet earth is watching the signs in the heavens that are dramatically increasing in number and intensity." The truth is, "America's best scientists" can't even agree on who the "best" *are*, much less would they jump on board Hagee's crazy train. As I will say more than once in this book: my brother is a professor of astronomy and he can assure you that Hagee's theories are not the least bit scientific in method. It is fraudulent for Hagee to imply, as he does repeatedly, that NASA endorses his theories.
•Hagee also wrote of the years **1492**, **1949** and **1967**, "Those three dates were the most important dates in all of Israel's history!" If he had not said "most" and added the exclamation point, we might give him the benefit of the doubt and call the statement just an exaggeration— instead of the outright lie that it is. Ask any Jewish historian, "What are the three most important dates in Jewish history?" Hagee would be lucky if even one of his dates made the list. More significant dates include: c.a. **1312 BC**, Moses' exodus from Egypt; c.a. **597 BC**, the first Babylonian Exile; **70 AD**: the

fall of Jerusalem, the Temple razed by Rome, and the start of *The Diaspora*; **1099 AD**, Crusaders capture Jerusalem; **1938**, *Kristallnacht* and the beginning of the Nazi holocaust; **1945**, the liberation of Jews from the concentration camps; **1979**, Egyptian-Israeli peace treaty signed. Indeed, Perry Stone, in his own book on the topic (*Deciphering End-Time Prophetic Codes*), proposes an entirely different list of "important" Jewish dates: **71 AD, 1453 AD, 1917 AD**.

Finally, from a Christian perspective, would not **4 BC** be a more significant date than any of the three dates cited by Hagee? Four BC marks the birth of the long-prophesied Jewish Messiah. Christians call Jesus THE King of the Jews, so to omit His birth from the list of most important dates is quite odd for a preacher like Hagee.

Hagee uses none of those dates because, inconveniently, they don't match the dates of any of his blood moon eclipses. Even the dates of the events he does cite often must be ***stretched*** to match. Stretching a date in this matter of exact counts and numerical reckonings is the same as stretching the truth, especially considering that Hagee's theory portrays God as a detailed micro-manager, in full control of world events, pre-setting every human action in advance. Setting aside the question of human free will, Hagee's understanding of God is self-contradicting. If God the Master of Details were trying to send us numerical codes, God the Perfect Accountant should have done a much more accurate job of it. A Hagee-described God should have made the lunar eclipse happen in 1492, not 1493, because the Alhambra Decree, expelling Jews from Spain, happened in 1492. But Hagee tries to fudge and nudge the date into the 1493-1494 period of eclipses. Why didn't God force the tetrad to occur in 1478, when King Ferdinand *first* initiated the Spanish Inquisition? Or if God didn't want to tinker with the movements of the moon, perhaps God should have delayed the King from his order. God is not very cooperative with Hagee's theory.

When Moons Collide

I find it humorous, despite the fact the End Time propheteers routinely steal ideas from each other, how often their own pet "systems" conflict. Hagee's Blood Moon system has no room in it to list the beginning of the Holocaust, the 1938 *Kristallnacht*, because there is no associated Blood Moon. But Jonathan Cahn's "Shemitah" system must insist on pointing to it, because 1938 is a Shemitah year. Cahn calls it "The Fateful Year," but Hagee ignores it. Both systems can't be right—because their key dates conflict—and I will argue that, in fact, both systems are wrong!

One more obvious problem with Hagee's "most important dates" list: how about 1948, instead of 1949? The rebirth of the Jewish nation, the signing of Israel's "Declaration of Independence," happened over a year before Hagee's "sign in the heavens" eclipse tetrad of 1949-1950. He even admits, in the same book, that "Israel" was "reborn May 1948...." So how does an event a year *later* serve as a "sign"? It would be as if I claimed a comet streaking across the sky in December 1777 was a direct sign from God predicting July 4th, 1776. Or put another way: What if I were selling "silver commemorative 4th of July Independence Day coins" inscribed with November 18th, 1777... how many would I sell? Or another: What good would it do you if I gave you a "prophetic warning" *today* that your house burned down *yesterday*? Close only counts in horseshoes and hand grenades. One year off may not seem like much to Hagee, but one number off can cost you a million in the Lotto.

Nitpicking?

Another quick counter-rebuttal to those who may accuse me of nit-picking about dates being a year off: Hagee *et al.* boast of deciphering an exactness in prophecy that simply can't be found in Scripture. Scholars decisively agree on the precise dating of less than a handful of events in the Bible. Even the most conservative Bible literalists argue over dates. Yet, "exact" is the word Hagee chooses to assert. In *Four Moons* he writes, "It is very rare that Scripture, science and historical events align with one another, yet the last three Four Blood Moon series or Tetrads have done exactly that." *Exactly* that? Even if we ignore the fact that Joel's prophecy was already fulfilled in Acts 2, the *only* remaining date of the three Tetrads that Hagee gets anywhere near "exactly" right in matching eclipses with an event is 1967, the Six Days War. Though admittedly a huge victory for Israel, it consisted only of a few battles, not a protracted war. Few Jewish historians, in the long history of Israel, would place its significance in the Top Three Most Important, as Hagee does. He had to overrate the event to fit his purposes. I imagine he would have picked any one of the *scores* of wars and battles we could list from six thousand years of Jewish history if it would fit some astronomical event. But all he could find was **one** event—the brief battles of 1967—making this "alignment" merely a statistically- unsurprising coincidence. To again quote a well-worn aphorism: even a blind pig stumbles on an acorn now and then.

Other tetrads that fell on Jewish holidays—about half of the total—did not match any significant date in Jewish history. Biltz admits this.

Shemitah Insignificance

When it suits him, Hagee will sometimes try to make a "Shemitah" year seem significant. He makes a feeble effort to show significance for the Shemitah year of 1994, but all he could do was match it with "Yassar Arafat returned to Palestine." In the long run, the event was insignificant to the Jews: Arafat failed to establish a Palestinian state, was replaced as head of the PLO, and died having achieved very little.

Speaking of Shemitahs, let me add here that the same kind of inconsistent over-reaching is found in Jonathan Cahn's work. He tries to claim that Shimitah years mark the rise of American power via the two World Wars: "Both 1917 and 1945 stand as key turning points in American and world history. They share, as well, another distinction: each is the Year of the Shemitah. America's rise to world superpower begins with one Shemitah and [was] completed with another."[6] One problem here is that 1917 is when the U.S. **entered** WWI, and 1945 is when we **ended** WWII. It is possible that exact *opposite* events (starting a war vs. finishing a war) signify the same thing (American hegemony), but it is more likely an example of Cahn desperately trying to wedge all events into the nearest Shemitah year. You can bet that if the Shemitah year had been at the end of WWI, late 1918, he would have cited *that* as the significant event (just as he did with the ending of WWII). But historians do not even agree about when to date the rise of American power; many would cite the Spanish-American war, not WWI.

Cahn also tries to tie war events of 1973 with the Shemitah of that year. He rhetorically asks, "What year did America lose its first war in modern times? It happened in 1973, the Year of the Shemitah.... [Our] nation would suffer its first military defeat in modern history." He is referring to the Viet Nam War. But did we really "lose [our] first war... in 1973." No. The Paris Peace Accords were signed in 1973, but this was not a surrender, it was a mutually-agreed upon ceasefire. Viet Nam was no more of a surrender than the Korean Armistice in the Fifties, so if you choose to call a ceasefire a "defeat," then Korea, not Nam, was our "first military defeat." And in fact, we did not remove the last of our troops until 1975, when Saigon fell; 1975 marks our "defeat" as much or more so than 1973. But that doesn't fit neatly into Cahn's scenario.

Considering the number of possible dates and events one could list of significance in world history, these are surprisingly-dismal matches. Cahn's stretched correlations do not make a convincing argument that these are planned signs from God. Jewish history is international in scope (cultural, religious and ethnic Jewish groups dot the globe), so even in the centuries that the nation of Israel did not exist, there were plenty of notable dates/events to pick from. And of course, all the writers add the United States into the mix, viewing it as the New Israel… so the list of "significant" dates on the Israeli and American timeline is nearly limitless.

Calendar Conundrum

At a more basic level, the absurdity of trying to match events and predict dates/years is proven when we realize how arbitrary our calendar dating system is in the first place. In 46 BC, Julius Caesar authorized that a calendar year be set at 365.25 days. While fairly-accurate, the Julian calendar still did not match the reality of earth's orbit, and over time the given date versus the real astronomical date (the solar calendar) came to vary by about ten days. So in 1582, Pope Gregory instituted a revision, establishing the Gregorian calendar we use today, which added leap years to fix the problem. The Gregorian calendar is also predicated on Year Zero as the birth of Christ, which now most scholars instead place at 4 BC, so do we deduct four years from every date? And the Jewish calendar uses a completely different numbering system. What all this means is that the date I'm writing these words in 2015 is not actually connected to Bible dates or prophecies with any mathematical precision. Trying to align Shemitahs with specific events/eclipses in numerically-symbolic ways is a flawed exercise from the start. Most of the End Time propheteers probably know this, which is why they include disclaimers. Cahn, for example, writes that "the focus of the message is not date-setting."

Then he, like the others, proceeds unabated to focus on date-setting.

Based on past history, once their projected "significant dates" of 2015 come and go without incident, I don't expect the propheteers to apologize or retract. Most likely they will then just look for another future date and write another book claiming a connection to a Bible sign or code. There does not seem to be much incentive for humility or *mea culpa*'s among the End Times writers, because the publishing contracts just keep coming.

~~~

Chapter Four: *The Glass is Half Empty*
The Danger of Doomsday Pessimism

"Jesus answered: 'Watch out that no one deceives you. For many will come in my name, claiming, 'I am the Messiah,' and will deceive many. You will hear of wars and rumors of wars, but see to it that you are not alarmed. Such things must happen, but the end is still to come.'"
~*Matthew 24:4-6*

"These things I have spoken unto you, that in me ye might have peace. In the world ye shall have tribulation: but be of good cheer; I have overcome the world."
~*John 16:33 KJV*

Does dark doomsday despair serve the Christian cause, or does it drive people away from the faith by peddling pessimism rather than hope? Jesus commanded us to "be of good cheer," that in Him is "peace" (John 16:33). He also warned us to not be "alarmed" by deceitful "rumors" (Matthew 24:4-6).

We are not idiot-children. We do not need to be chastised and warned that life is risky, that storms may come, that bad things can happen to good people. Most of us, if we lived many years or studied history a few years, know all too well that we must be prepared for calamity. As Dr. Scott Peck put it so pithily: "Life is difficult."

The majority of End Time propheteers make it their mission to paint with the broadest and blackest strokes. Offer warnings if you must, you who see yourself as modern-day Jeremiahs, but don't LIE to us. Describing a half-full glass as half-empty is your prerogative, I suppose… but to describe that same half-full glass as completely dry is deceptive fearmongering.

When Urgent Takes Thirty Years

Irvin Baxter is the founder of Endtime Ministries, which

produces radio, TV and print media all for the purpose of warning the world, especially Israel, of the soon-coming End of Time. He's had that urgent warning going for over thirty years. Urgently. Warning. Any day now.

Baxter's End Times website doesn't keep long records of his failed predictions over the years, but we can find there his response to 2012 news headlines about troubles in Syria and Iran. His sidekick Dave cites these banner headlines: "WAR IN WEEKS" and "Syria's Assad Threatens to Start World War III." That was three years ago. Fizzle. In 2007, Baxter stated in print, "I believe two billion people will die in the next 12 months."[7] That's a good way to sell his DVD sets at over a hundred bucks, because paper money will be worthless when WWIII begins. He added that "it certainly seems probable that the prophesied apocalypse will occur while [George W. Bush] is yet in office." That was over eight years ago. Fizzle. But Irvin still states ominously, "The question is not, 'Is there going to be a World War III?' It is in your Bible.... Another world war is coming, and it will be the biggest world war ever.... This war that is coming will kill 2.2 billion, forty times World War II."[8] His site warns, "At the very least you should store up enough non-perishable food and water." Surprisingly, I don't see survival kits for sale on his website; he's missing a marketing opportunity. If you look up "fearmonger" in the dictionary, there should be a picture of Irvin Baxter under it.

Of course, we can also use Hagee again as another example. Consider his section in *Four Blood Moons* that warns of a coming famine. It begins with the title, "The Demise of the Family Farm."

The Famine is Coming... or Not

Hagee is certain that the loss of the idyllic small family farm has already sown seeds of famine (an ironical metaphor). I don't take issue with all of his statistics; no question, most small family farms have been replaced by huge corporate operations—farm factories. I lament that. My grandfather and my uncles were small-size farmers. But frankly, Hagee's lament is akin to mourning the decline of buggy-whip manufacturing. Other than an accompanying horse-unemployment problem, the world was not harmed when buggy-whip manufacturing phased out. And while we might pine for the romance of the independent mom and pop farm, we are not even remotely in danger of famine in the developed world. While Hagee details his dark list of how bad things are down on the farm, he never once mentions that we now feed billions— far, far more than during the hay-day of the family farm. Hagee also fails to mention that we aren't having a repeat of the dustbowl of the twenties (he forgets that dark period of family farming) because of modern soil conservation methods. Nor does he mention the effective hybrids that now yield bumper crops, with less pesticides, nor does he acknowledge we have better preservatives and better methods of food storage, nor does he own up to the fact that food is, these days, available in far greater variety for far less cost (as a percentage of real income) than ever in human history. Overall, the state of modern agriculture is a golden age. **But that doesn't fit the script of the End Time pessimists.** No, instead Hagee whines: "The famine is coming. It's just a matter of time." And by that, he means worldwide, unrelenting, longterm starvation. Scary stuff. Until you look at the facts. So again, Hagee is caught in a complete fabrication without an iota of scientific support.

The Death Tax Lie

Incidentally, Hagee tells another lie in this section, claiming that the IRS "death tax can exceed 50 percent of a farm's total value" and the tax is "lurking in the wings hastening the demise of the American farm." This is, first of all, an outright lie. Second, it is part of the Republican agenda: to smear the idea of taxing wealthy estates, to induce fear, to play on our sympathies for the brave family farmer, all for the cynical purpose of ensuring that the ultra-rich, like Hagee, get to hang onto every inch of their largesse. Hagee has a personal bias, too, as he has a huge farm, in a Trust so that it is largely exempt from *all* taxes. Of course, speaking of exemptions, that's a big part of Hagee's lie regarding ALL farms: he fails to mention the exemption, which for a couple is $10.86 million in 2015.

The truth is only a handful of small family-owned farms owe any estate tax, and even the largest are never going to lose anything remotely close to "50 percent of a farm's total value," as Hagee asserts. In the entire nation, only twenty small business and farm estates owed *any* estate tax in 2013, according to the Tax Policy Center.[9] And that's not tiny one-mule farms, it includes those with farm or business assets valued at up to $5 million. The punchline is that the Tax Policy Center estimates those 20 estates owed less than 5% of their value in tax, on average. These findings are consistent with a 2005 Congressional Budget Office (CBO) study finding that of the few farm and family business estates that would owe any estate tax in 2009, the overwhelming majority would have sufficient liquid assets in the estate to pay the tax without having to touch the farmland or business. Since then, estate tax rules have become even more favorable for taxpayers. Special estate tax law provisions allow families to spread tax payments over a 15-year period, with low interest rates. Let us remember that every year (not just at death), farmers enjoy their own set of loopholes and deductions, including a huge property tax break. Many wealthy estates employ teams of lawyers and accountants to exploit loopholes in the estate tax in order to pass on most of their estates untouched. As icing on the cake, in most cases, the million dollar farms Hagee is concerned about have enjoyed generous agricultural subsidies— handouts—from the U.S. Department of Agriculture and state governments across the years. A meager "death tax" is the least thing a farmer has to worry about. It is absurd for Hagee to blame the "demise of the family farm" on government. This may seem unrelated to our topic, but it speaks to his total lack of credibility. And he is not alone: most of these writers have a political bias and an exaggerated pessimism that skews their objectivity. We will examine the issue of political bias further in Chapter Ten.

Jonathan Cahn's Dark Warnings

Another dark pessimist is Jonathan Cahn. Cahn is sure that America is headed for economic calamity of the most dire, disastrous kind. Reading his work can make you either want to sell all your stock and buy survival kits, or commit suicide. Before we look at his specialty of "economic fearmongering," let's look generally at whether his "Shemitah" methods have any validity in the broadest sense.

Cahn, like most prophecy prognosticators, believes he can predict the future even down to the hour (even though the Bible, which he swears devotion to, explicitly states no one can predict the future... see Ecclesiastes 8:7). He boasts that his Shemitah system can "pinpoint the exact time, down to dates and hours, of some of the most critical events in modern times." That's a bold claim, and though Cahn tries at another point in his book to back away from such exactitude, he can't help himself and again speaks of a "precision" in his prophecies that "set the time and dates...."

Apocamandering

The problem with Cahn's theories is that they are "gerrymandered" to match dates with events, in much the same way that Hagee fudges his blood moon date-to-event "matches." For those who have forgotten their 10th Grade Civics lesson, "gerrymandering" was the pejorative term applied to the unethical political practice of distorting natural or established borders of voting districts in ways that would be beneficial to a particular Party. An early effort by Governor Gerry of Massachusetts re-drew a map of the congressional district into the shape of a salamander (thus Gerry-mander) to clump-in enough voters of his party to win the election. I am hereby coining the term "**apocamander**" to describe the practice by apocalyptic writers of redrawing reality to fit their pet End Time theories. "Apocamandering" is the dubious act of stretching and distorting historical dates/events and Bible verses in such a way as to create an unnatural overlap, to create the appearance of a significant correlation where there is none.

Here are some more examples of *apocamandering*:
•Cahn cites two "Shemitah years" as crucial in the history of the U.S. by claiming they are when we established our world dominance: 1917 and 1945. The problem is, 1917 is when the U.S. *entered* World War I, and 1945 is when we *ended* World War II. Which is it? Which establishes dominance: *entering* a war or *ending* a war? Cahn wants it both ways because that's the only way it fits his Shemitah system! These kinds of *apples to oranges* false comparisons can be found in many of the End Times books, as they stretch history to fit their needs.
•Hagee looks at Blood Moons dates not just as a single *day* of a lunar eclipse, but expands his target to a period of 18 or more *months*. Likewise, Cahn expands his Shemitah targets. He speaks of "the Shemitah's approach," then its "midst," then its "wake." What that actually means is that the year before, the year of, and the year after a Shemitah are fair game for Cahn's shot. He has thus created **a three year window of seeming significance**. An important historical event doesn't have to land exactly on a specific Shemitah year; if it is *anywhere* within the three year window, Cahn claims it to be significant. His chief talent is to write and

present things in such a way that we fail to notice this sleight of hand. An example: Cahn sees grand significance in the construction of the World Trade Center twin towers' replacement, the "Freedom Tower." He writes: "At the end of 2006 the ground was cleared to begin the foundation. In 2007 came the preparing of the foundation. At the beginning of 2008 the building's core began rising, ultimately to reach street level. The Shemitah was 2007–2008. Though the foundation and preparatory work began earlier, the rising of the tower began in the Year of the Shemitah."[10] By his own admittance, the construction began in 2006, long before the 2007-2008 Shemitah, and the tower wasn't completed until 2013… so his attempt to correlate either the groundbreaking or the completion with his Shemitah is a sham.

•Yet another example is in Cahn's linking the Great Depression with a Shemitah. He writes: "Shemitah took place in 1930–1931. More specifically, the Shemitah began in late 1930—the same time the world economy began its steady deterioration." But the Great Depression began in **1929**, with widespread panic in the Stock Market and all-time record losses. All the foundational damage was done in 1929, and the rest of the Depression was a slow recovery after that. So of what use would the **1930-31** Shemitah be as a prophetic warning of an event that began—and hit its hardest—in the Panic of **1929**? Speaking of "panic," it is more likely that economic doomsdayists like Cahn, Hagee, etc., could *trigger* an economic panic before they would ever accurately *predict* one!

Indeed, the main focus of Cahn's book, *The Mystery of the Shemitah*, is to look at economic "disasters" in the U.S., and to try to match those up with the years of his Shemitah "cycle of sevens." The problem is, when we look at stock market crashes, depressions and significant recessions in U.S. history, they do not clump together at the seventh year marks. Not at all. So when **years** won't work, Cahn then tries to match stock market crashes with one of two "meaningful" **months** on the Hebrew calendar. He expands his target (a crash) by talking about its aftermath (ongoing recession).

If You Miss the Target, Just Make a Bigger Target

In the case of the 9-11 attacks in 2001, Cahn expands the target time by including the days the NY stock exchange was frozen (closed) *after* the attacks. Even with his expanded times to allow a "target hit" and with his shift from a 7th year focus to a two-months- out-of-twelve focus, Cahn still calls a 60% matchup "remarkable" and a "mind-boggling phenomenon." Remember, predicting a flip of a coin always results in a 50% match-up! So he thinks it is remarkable to point to something that ranks 10% higher than mere coincidence. Moreover, this reference to a post 9-11 crash is based on what *he* chooses to label the Top Ten biggest market crashes lining up with what he deems the two significant months on the Jewish calendar, Elul and Tishri. He might as well say, "See! *This 'n that* line-up... in one way or another... sorta... at least, as close as horseshoes and hand-grenades." Personally, for my mind to be "boggled," I would need to see more like an 80% or 90% coordinated line-up... what's the point of **a tad more than half** lining up with something as broad as an entire month? One more metaphor: it's like someone playing darts and bragging, "Look at my accuracy, I hit *somewhere* on the dart board 60% of the time!" If you can hit the *bulls-eye* 60% of the time, I might be impressed, or if you could hit the dartboard, at any location, *100%* of the time, that too would be a decent darts thrower. But Cahn can't even hit wide on the dartboard much better than half of the time. Sometimes it seems like he threw the dart and *then* drew the target around it! He can't show an exact and to-the-day match of market crashes with, for example, a Jewish festival. His Shemitah gauge (1930-1931) was a *year* late in predicting the 1929 crash. I would assume,

in Cahn's theology, that God would want His people to avoid losing their life savings, so what "warning" of a the crash a year after it happened does not at all seem "remarkable."
Heck, if God is trying to give us a symbolic "harbinger," why can't there be a stock market crash lined up with the 7th Year Shemitah *and* with a special Tishri month *and* a blood moons eclipse...in advance? Even the odds of that are not as "remarkable" as one might think: there are only 365 days in a year, so the odds of something significant happening on any given day are only 365 to 1. That may seem like tall odds, but the average Powerball lottery has odds of 1 in 175,223,510... and *somebody* wins that match-up! A key difference between a lottery winner and an End Time predictor is that, while both are subject to unknown random numbers, the lottery bettor is an optimist, while the End Time Chicken Little is a pessimist… betting on disaster.

The Sky is Falling... or Maybe an Acorn

The End Time writers failed to learn a lesson from the children's parable, "Chicken Little." When an acorn fell on her head, Chicken Little (Henny Penny in some versions) ran about screaming to her friends, "The sky is falling." They joined in her irrational panic and decided to go warn the king, but on the way, Foxy-Loxy takes them to his den and eats them. (A lot of fables scare the hell out of little kids… what's up with that!?) The tale is one of irony: the world was NOT ending, but because of irrational panic, bad things did befall Chicken Little.

My fear about the dire economic warnings found in End Times books is that they could become a **self-fulfilling prophecy**. The erosion of consumer confidence has already, historically, proven to be harmful to economies. This is exactly why economists call a Crash, such as the 1929 Black Tuesday event, a "Panic."

In addition to Hagee's ridiculous "sky is falling" rant about farms and famines, consider these exhibits of over-stating economic calamity. Cahn writes: "On the fourth Shemitah… in 1973, [the post-war financial] order would suffer collapse. That same year would begin a long-term financial collapse that would combine with one of the most severe economic recessions in [our] history."[11]

Sorry, but the world did not even come close to a "financial collapse" in the Seventies. Oil prices rose significantly, triggering inflation, and the U.S. fell into a relatively short-lived recession. But the rate of inflation was nowhere near the hyperinflation seen in Weimar Germany in the Twenties, or in South America in the Eighties. Our economy churned on, and by 1975, the recession ended and the economy began growing again. At the very worst of the 1973-74 downturn, unemployment never rose above 10% (compared to 25% during the Great Depression); there were no bread lines, no massive hardship in the U.S. In fact, it was one of the most short-lived recessions.[12] But anything that happens in a Shemitah year is, for Cahn, a disaster and a "collapse."   He might wish to look up the word "collapse" ("to fall in; to fail completely"). The Great Depression, and maybe even the Crash of 2008, could be called a financial collapse, but the downturns of 1973 and 2001 did not destroy or derail our economy. And in fact, the mini-crash of NASDAQ that he cites occurred in March 2000—*not* in the Shemitah year of 2001. Yes, the 2007-2008 Crash *was* partly in a Shemitah year, and it was the worst U.S. economic calamity since the Great Depression. But even with 2008, hurtful as it was to pensioners' retirement funds, those who resisted the urge to sell saw most of their stocks rebound in a few years, and within six years, the market hit all time highs even as unemployment fell to below 6%. Again, there were no riots in the street or bread lines down the block in 2001 or even 2008. The bigger point is that one significant Shemitah-date coincidence in the 200 year history of the U.S. economy is *insignificant* in the big picture.

There is nothing in Cahn's book to convince me of any divine match-up between stock market crashes and particular Jewish holy days/years. If there were, Cahn should be rich from investing in the market, not from writing best-sellers.

Spurious Correlations

The slight statistical cluster that he can point to—that a majority of stock market crashes have occurred in September and October, near the time of Jewish harvest festivals—is an interesting anomaly. But I find nothing in the Bible that makes me think God is manipulating the market. There are several simple, non-supernatural explanations. First, many companies report their financial year-end earnings in October. If a company underperforms expectations early in a year, the market is more forgiving... but less so at the calendar winds down. Also, October is a time that brokers tend to sell-off some mutual funds for profit-taking purposes that have to do with the timing of fiscal reporting, not with Jewish festivals.

The Autumn phenomenon also has psychological reasons. Lily Fang, a professor at MIT, has studied the fact that there is a statistical "blip" of stock market sell-offs in Septembers and Octobers. She thinks it is mostly a factor of the lifestyle of financial traders. They have the kind of fat incomes and cushy time-off that allows them to take a lot of weeks away from the office during the summer holidays. The traders and investors are often buoyed by those halcyon days of summer, plus they have less time to focus on financial market news. Then when they return to their offices in September, they begin to "sober up," digest any bad financial news, and start looking ahead to the end of the year, whereupon they realize the small economic clouds they had been able to shrug off whilst on holiday are now looking more like thunderstorms. Then panic can set in.

Economics professor Stephen Williamson argues that there's little evidence to suggest the next big crash will occur in October. He states: "Stock market crashes have occurred sufficiently infrequently in history that there is not enough [statistically-meaningful] evidence on when they are more likely to occur." Williamson adds: "Crashes could be completely random events," but since the history of the stock market is relatively short, and "there are few [crashes], there is a high probability" that they happen in clusters without that having any true statistical meaning or cause. This is what scientists call "spurious correlation," random events that only have the *appearance* of meaning but which fail to hold up as significant over longer periods of time.

So Cahn has stumbled onto a "phenomenon," alright... the two-fold phenomenon of human psychology that **1.** the human eye tends to see that which it looks for and **2.** the human mind tends to try to find order in things, even to the point of imposing order. The technical terms are **1.** *pareidolia* and **2.** *apophenia*, which we will revisit in the next chapter... but for now:

1. If I ask you to find a bunny and a man's face in the clouds, chances are high you could find them if you stared long enough. I also notice that whenever I buy a new car of a specific model and color, I begin to spot many other people driving the same type/color car. The End Times authors are constantly and intently looking for specific correlations (i.e. signs), so they **usually find what they are looking for.**

2. We impose order even where there is mostly randomness. Pour out the tiles from your Scrabble game, flip the tiles letter up, and stare at the unsorted letters. Chances are high you'll start seeing words. If the letters happen to roughly line up to spell, *"Shoot yourself,"* please understand that is not a mystical instruction. It is a random occurrence, a spurious correlation. Relax. Instead, keep stirring and studying the Scrabble tiles and eventually you will see the words *"God* *says to live."*

Optimism is a Christian Virtue

Any good and significant improvement to the human condition usually began with positive thinking and optimism. A dark fatalism, a belief or fear that the world will end soon in an unavoidable conflagration, conversely is a dream-killer. If a young person comes to believe the world is ending next year, why go to college? If persuaded that a new holocaust is on the horizon, what entrepreneur would waste energies building a company, what inventor would put in the studious hours to work out a world-changing invention, what medical researcher would waste time buried in the laboratory to find a cure for cancer? Book a trip to Disneyworld or a vacation in Hawaii. Heck, get a second mortgage on the house and take the cash for a wild week in Vegas!

My comments are exaggerated, but the underlying truth is that those who are obsessed with End Times live with a shadowy theology that assumes all human efforts are in vain. You may agree with King Solomon, that "all is vanity," but please understand that is an Old Testament view. The view of the New, the teachings of Jesus and Paul, encourage us to be positive thinkers filled with optimism for life in the here and now as well as in the coming Kingdom of Heaven. Jesus said, "The Kingdom of God is in your midst," (Luke 17:21). He taught, "...do not worry about tomorrow.... Each day has enough trouble of its own." (Matthew 6:34). Paul said, "Whatever is noble, whatever is right, whatever is pure, whatever is lovely, whatever is admirable—if anything is excellent or praiseworthy—think about such things." (Philippians 4:8)

Watching videos and reading books about the atrocities of the antichrist and the horrors of a world war, with the death of two billion people (according to evangelist Irvin Baxter), is clearly counter to Paul's advice. Paul, who never let the threat of persecution slow him from living an active, fruitful life, wrote that "...those who live in accordance with the Spirit have their minds set on what the Spirit desires... the mind governed by the Spirit is life and peace." (Romans 8:5-6, excerpts) And long before the Roman poet Horace Flaccus said, "Carpe Diem!" (Seize the day!), the Psalmist urged us similarly: "This is the day that the Lord has made; let us rejoice and be glad in it!"

~~~

Chapter Five:
The Rumors of Our Death Are Greatly Exaggerated
Failed Predictions of Hal Lindsey and Friends

"Since no one knows the future, who can tell someone else what is to come?"
 ~*Ecclesiastes 8:7*

"You will hear of wars and rumors of wars—but don't be alarmed. Such things must happen, but that is not the end."
 ~*Jesus, in Matthew 24:6 (J.B. Phillips trans.)*

Most baby boomers became familiar with the concepts of Rapture, Tribulation, Armageddon, etc., through the best-selling book of the early seventies with a eulogy for a title: *The Late, Great Planet Earth*, by Hal Lindsey. To paraphrase Mark Twain, the rumors of the end of the world have been greatly exaggerated... so many times that the "boy who cried wolf" should be given a pardon by comparison! Wikipedia details well over a hundred "prophets" and their 100+ failed predictions.[13]

The Late, Never-Great, Lindsey

We will look at that list in a moment, but first let's consider how often the "godfather" of the modern End Times movement, **Hal Lindsey**, was wrong:

•Lindsey predicted that the world would run out of raw materials by 1986, and that by the end of the 1980's, the Arab nations would have a complete stranglehold on energy. (Today OPEC is begging for mercy, a barrel of oil is under a hundred bucks, and oil imports are at an all-time low in the U.S.)

•In 1979, Lindsey announced that the antichrist had already been born in Europe and would appear on the world stage in the mid-Eighties.

•Lindsey predicted an all out nuclear world war would hit

before 1989
- Lindsey predicted that the 1982 "Jupiter Effect" (a partial planetary alignment) would cause worldwide disaster. He predicted "the largest outbreak of killer quakes ever seen in the history of planet earth." To the contrary, there were *fewer* major earthquakes than average that year.
- Lindsey predicted that the European Union would be the most powerful nation in the world before 1990. Today, the EU is held together by bailing wire and duct tape.
- Lindsey predicted the murder of all Mormons. He failed to predict a Mormon getting nearly 50% of the vote for President in 2012.
- Lindsey predicted that a super-powerful Russia would invade Jerusalem in the 1980's, and he failed to predict the break-up of the USSR. Instead, he wrote: "The current [1970] build-up of Russian ships in the Mediterranean serves as another significant sign of the possible nearness of Armageddon."[14]
- Lindsey called the Eighties the "countdown to Armageddon." Ten, nine, eight, seven... stand by, Houston, we have a problem.

It must be nice to sell 40 million copies of a book that has been utterly disproven—and still get to keep the money! He was never one to stop at being wrong repeatedly. For over forty years, Lindsey keeps pumping out his pulp fiction. In 1998, he came out with, *Planet Earth: The Final Chapter*, but alas, it was not his *final* chapter, as yet more books came after that. Apparently the only way to stop Hal's repeated attempts at soothsaying is for the End to actually come. Sorry, Hal, but history just keeps going and going....

1948 Clock Runs Out; Hal Lindsey Loses; New Team in Overtime

As of 2015, most of what the famous writer Hal Lindsey had predicted—insisted—would come to pass **has not**. As

Lindsey's credibility has slowly faded, other writers and evangelists have been eager to jump into the game... so many, in fact, that I won't have space here to examine them all. A few examples:

End Times evangelist **Perry Stone** claims that God speaks to him routinely in dreams with visions of the future. He tries to gloss over the colossal mistake that End Times authors have been trumpeting for the last half a century or so: that Israel's rebirth in 1948 started a tick-tock countdown, and that it would be within that "generation" that Christ would return. And according to the evangelical view, a "generation" was Jewish-speak for a 40 years period. The window has now passed. Perry Stone, having bought into that biblical view held by Lindsey and others like him, had to deal with their prediction that Jesus would return by 1998, or at the very least, Tribulation would begin—based on the 1948 restoration of Israel plus 40 years. So he now states that a generation is somewhere between 50 and 100 years. But to quote Hal Lindsey: "A generation in the Bible is something like forty years.... within forty years or so of 1948, all these things could take place. Many scholars who have studied Bible prophecy all their lives believe that this is so."[15] When 1988 came and went, some began to change their definition of a biblical "generation," and pointed out that an average lifespan, at the time the prophecies were given, was actually more like 70 years. 1948 plus 70 equals 2018—which gave them more time to sell books. But to say that most of a generation would be alive to witness all the events is getting harder and harder to "sell." And considering the events surrounding the End Times, Tribulation, Armageddon, etc. all told would take nearly a decade to completely unfold, they are having to re-jigger yet again these days. In his 2008 book, *Living In The Final Chapter*, Perry Stone backpedals: "It is obvious now that" the Scripture did not apply to the 1948 generation, so, now "I believe [it is] the generation that saw Jerusalem re-united in *1967*..." that would see the End Times. He is referring to the fact that in the victory of the Six Day War in 1967, Israel tore down one of the walls that had divided the city. Of course, the city was not truly "re-united," because Muslims continue to control significant parts of Jerusalem, including the most holy Temple Mount. Nevertheless, re-setting the Doomsday Clock to 1967 and re-numbering a generation as anywhere from 50 to 70 years has given the prognosticating writers many more decades in which to sell books, CD's and DVD's before people discover they are wrong (yet again).

Hagee, however, has doubled-down with his Blood Moons theory by again speeding up the timetable. We will know he was wrong much, much sooner than his predecessors (September 2015). Perhaps he can take comfort in remembering he has plenty of company.

Failure upon Failure

As we continue our list of failed prophets, from fairly notable and/or highly educated writers and leaders across the years, and their many failed predictions, do remember my list is only a partial sampling:

• Evangelist **Charles Taze Russell**, founder of the *Jehovah's Witness* denomination, wrote that "...the battle of the great day of God Almighty" was "definitely" marked in Scripture as October 1914. (It definitely didn't happen.)

• The *Jehovah's Witness* folks took another stab at it and predicted the End for 1941.

• **Herbert W. Armstrong**, the founder of the so-called *Worldwide Church of God*, warned members of his church that the Rapture would happen in 1936. After that year came and went, he changed the date three more times before giving up on a specific date.[16]

• Celebrity Prophetess **Jeanne Dixon** predicted the world would end in 1962. She failed to predict her own death from cardiac arrest in 1997. She had also predicted the Russians would be the first to land on the moon.

•For **Rev. Jim Jones** and the *People's Temple*, the magic date of nuclear holocaust would be 1967. Ironically, he never "drank the Kool-Aid," but apparently waited to kill himself with a gun in 1978.

•In 1976, **Pat Robertson** predicted Jesus would come by 1983. In 1980 and in 1982, Robertson said the Tribulation would begin in 1982: "I guarantee you by the fall of 1982 that there is going to be a judgment on the world... by the fall, undoubtedly... this will happen which will fulfill Ezekiel."[17] Ezekiel speaks of the battle of Armageddon, brought about by Gog and Magog, which the End Times writers were sure was Russia. Wrong on all counts. Robertson later revised it to say the End Times trouble would start with the year 2000, a rather unoriginal idea shared by many others, including **Tim LaHaye, Jerry Falwell**, and even **Sir Isaac Newton**. And we've already seen that Hal Lindsey never imagined, when he wrote *The Late, Great Planet Earth*, that our tired old planet would still be fine and dandy way past 2001.

•Add to the list these names discussed elsewhere in this book: **William Miller, John Darby, Cyrus Scofield, Edgar C. Whisenant, Billy Graham, and Tim LaHaye**. If we had space and interest, we could examine many more recent failed prognosticators: **Harold Camping, Leo Harris, Leon Bates, Barry Smith, Jonathan Cahn, David Jeremiah, Robert Van Kampen, Dave Hunt, Grant R. Jeffrey**, *et cetera*, etc. All *wrong*.

Even less familiar to many readers is the fact that those names from the modern era are pre-dated by a great number of incorrect "prophets" from the prior two thousand years:

•**Hilary of Poitiers** announced that the end would happen in 365 AD.

•**Saint Martin of Tours** was convinced that the end would

happen before 400 AD.
- **Hippolytus** and **Sextus Julius Africanus** both predicted Armageddon for 500 AD.
- **German Emperor Otto III** bet on 968 AD.
- **Gerard of Poehlde** projected the world's end for 1306 CE.
- **John of Toledo** predicted the end of the world during 1186. This estimate was based on the alignment of many planets.
- **Joachim of Fiore** predicted the End would be around 1205.
- **Pope Innocent III** computed the date would be 1284 by adding 666 years onto the date that Islam was founded. Math is always such fun to play around with.
- **Melchior Hoffman** predicted that Jesus' return would happen a millennium and a half after the nominal date of his execution, in 1533.
- **Benjamin Keach**, a 17th century Baptist, predicted the end of the world for 1689.
- British mathematician **William Whitson** predicted a great world-ending flood similar to Noah's for 1736.
- **Charles Wesley**, who with his brother, John Wesley, founded the Methodist church, thought that Doomsday would occur in 1794.
- **Joseph Smith,** founder of the Church of Jesus Christ of Latter-day Saints (Mormons), made several predictions about the End Times, but by 1892, all of his "revelations" proved to be false.
- In the 1800's, **Ellen White**, founder of the Seventh Day Adventists movement, made many predictions of the timing of the end of the world. By 1901, all of her "revelations" proved to be false.

Do we see a pattern here?[18]

True Scholars vs. Sloppy Scholarship

What you will not find on this list are the names of moderate, well-educated Bible scholars from the best mainstream seminaries/universities. Unfortunately, those true scholars whose work has been verified by archeological discoveries (including the Dead Sea Scrolls) and by the best linguistic and contextual sciences, they are dismissed by many of the self-righteous John Hagee-types, who have a distrust of academics. Not only are their scholastic assertions dismissed, but many of the TV-evangelists also attack or question the scholars' faith, virtue and devotion to God. In answering them, I can also cherry-pick Bible quotes: "Beware of false prophets.... You will know them by their fruits." (Matthew 7:15-16).

Let's consider two more examples, one more famous for utilizing radio than books. Radio Preacher **Harold Camping** gained worldwide attention for "predicting" that the Rapture would happen on May 21st, 2011. Camping and his "ministry" made millions via his Family Radio network, and then spent—wasted—$100 million on a worldwide advertising campaign proclaiming Judgment Day. That's not a misprint: a tenth of a billion bucks, for nothing. This illustrates one of my complaints about End Times obsessions: a huge waste of money that helped no one and in fact resulted in derision and discredit. Sadly, some of his followers had sold all their worldly possessions to fund this boondoggle. He arrogantly asserted "without a shadow of a doubt" that Judgment Day would be on May 21st. The end result was that he was wrong, just as he was wrong when he had earlier mis-predicted the end would be September 6th, 1994, and wrong again when he tried to reconfigure his miscalculation a third time. Heck, he couldn't even predict his own demise in 2013 at 92.

The clearest example of failed arrogance is the late **Edgar C. Whisenant**. Here we have a self-described "Bible scholar" who was in many ways intelligent— a former NASA rocket engineer and a devoted student of Scriptural prophecy. But with that intelligence came a cockiness: Whisenant actually boasted, "Only if the Bible is in error am

I wrong." He left no room for backpedaling. His book was entitled, *88 Reasons Why the Rapture Will Be in 1988*, and each of the detailed reasons were a combination of *indisputable* mathematics and Scriptural knowledge. The only problem with his solid mathematics and divinely-inspired 88 "indisputable" assertions is that they WERE ALL WRONG! Every one. And he was not just wrong 88 times. When the Rapture failed to happen in September 1988, ("I would stake my life on" it, he had insisted), Whisenant was only slightly-humbled. Undaunted, he re-calculated and followed up with later books offering predictions for 1989, (failed), then 1993, (failed), then 1994, then 1997... just so he could be wrong that many more times. He also failed to foresee his own death in 2001.

It seems to me if you claim to predict the exact end of everyone on earth, you should at *least* be able to predict your own demise!

Apophenia and The Numbers Game

Reasons that End Times authors and prognosticators fail is that they don't check themselves, they don't consider alternative views, and they fall prey to a basic psychological problem underlying their methodology. By this, I mean **they fail to understand that the brain tries to find order in patterns** according to our pre-conceived assumptions. As I stated in the last chapter, if you look for a face in the clouds, you will find a face in the clouds. The scientific terms that have been coined for this include: *apophenia, patternicity and pareidolia*. There are detailed neurological reasons for these natural phenomena which are outside the scope of this book, but suffice it to say, it has been well-established as a scientific fact. I cite two sources for those readers interested: www.scientificamerican.com/article/patternicity-finding-meaningful-patterns/ and www.en.wikipedia.org/wiki/Apophenia. What *apophenia* means in a nutshell is this: our brains will tend to look for patterns in things, and we will err on the side of creating or imposing order—regardless of whether there is any real pattern in reality!

Some of those who try to jigger dates and numbers to indicate an "eerie significant coincidence" and deeper meaning are motivated by greed, but even the most sincere can still be affected by apophenia. The other fact that feeds these repeated failed predictions is that jiggering numbers is just all too easy to do!

As an example of apophenia: Perry Stone spends two entire chapters in his book searching for something supernatural and eerie with Presidential deaths. To understand the silliness behind this "numbers game," let's use a non-biblical example: the list of numeric coincidences between the assassinations of Presidents Lincoln and Kennedy. If you've never seen the list of comparisons, you may wish to Google it... at first glance, the list shows a compelling—to the point of seeming supernatural—synchronicity between the lives, and deaths, of the two Presidents.

- Abraham Lincoln was elected to Congress in 1846.
  John F. Kennedy was elected to Congress in 1946.
- Abraham Lincoln was elected President in 1860.
  John F. Kennedy was elected President in 1960.
- The names Lincoln and Kennedy each contain seven letters.
- Both Presidents were shot with a gun in the head..
- John Wilkes Booth was born in 1839.
  Lee Harvey Oswald was born in 1939. And more....

But a closer look shows that many of these numerical coincidences are not the least bit surprising or significant. First and foremost, whether in looking at the Lincoln/Kennedy correlation, or the alleged correlation of lunar events with dates, we must remember there are only ten digits (zero through nine) for *any* number combination, and there are only seven days in a week, 30 days in a month, and any given year has just 4 digits. This means we will *regularly* see matching numbers of two disparate events lining up in what looks like significant ways but are, mathematically, not strange at all. A person looking for mystical significance can select and manipulate numbers to force almost any two persons or events to appear connected numerically. For instance, with Lincoln and JFK, let's look at the supposedly-eerie fact that both were elected to Congress in '46, and both elected to the Presidency in '60. First, these elections were a *hundred* years apart—the numbers 1860 and 1960 don't have any abnormal mathematical connection and the "matching zeros" are not as "cool" as they may first appear. If we used a Chinese or Jewish calendar, the "matching zeros" would disappear; calendar dates are manmade artificialities. Moreover, Presidential elections, by design, only happen on *even* years, every four years, so it's not a statistically-significant coincidence that Lincoln was elected in 1860 and Kennedy in 1960. Neither of them could have run in '57, '58, '59, '61, '62 or '63, because there were no elections those years!

Much Ado about Nothing

Or consider this statement: "The names Lincoln and Kennedy each contain seven letters." The last names of Presidents Clinton and Johnson also have seven letters... it's a common length for a name. And never mind that their *first* names are not similar at all (Abraham vs. John). Almost ALL American names are going to be between four and eight letters long, so of course many will match in length. Yet, we are supposed to be amazed at such minor commonalities all the while ignoring the numerous **non**-coincidences. For example, Lincoln was born in 1809; Kennedy was born in 1917. Lincoln died in 1865; Kennedy died in 1963. Lincoln was 56 years old at the time of his death; Kennedy was 46 years old at the time of his death. Lincoln was a Republican, JFK was a Democrat. *Et cetera.* It goes beyond just numerical "coincidences": the observation that both were assassinated via gunshots to the head, is silly: almost *all* modern assassinations involve bullets to the head! No striking coincidence there. Even though the two men had a one in twelve chance of dying in the same month, we find no coincidence there, either: Lincoln was killed in April; Kennedy was killed in November. Also unmentioned here is the fact that Lincoln was re-elected to a second term as President, but Kennedy was killed in his *first* term. Lincoln first *saw* his assassin, actor John Wilkes Booth, in the theater in 1863, and Kennedy encountered his assassin in 1963. But Abe wasn't actually killed until 1865, and Jack never saw/met Oswald (or the Grassy Knoll shooter), so it's a contrived "coincidence."

With a little creativity, you can manipulate the numbers associated with just about any two events or persons. Finally, we must ask, what would be the cosmic significance of these perceived Lincoln/Kennedy parallels? Is it being suggested that God deviously planned and designed their lives (their names, their elections, their assassinations) and all the details, dates and players surrounding them, simply so we would go, "Ooooo, that's eerie and significant!"

I have also seen similar attempts to find mystical meaning regarding the 9-11 terrorist attacks of 2001. Eleven is supposedly a magic, evil number, so those who look for supernatural meanings point out that "9+1+1 equals 11." But this is "cooking the books"; it has no mathematical meaning. If anything, 9-11 might be considered "9 minus 11." And the date could just as easily be written as 9-11-01 (which equals 21 if added or -3 if subtracted), or 9-11-2001... none of those configurations equal 11. So we could, in hindsight, rig and jiggle the numbers of any date to line up with *something* significant that happened *somewhere* on the globe and go,

"Wow, that must be supernatural!"

As they said to Dr. Freud, "Sometimes a cigar is just a cigar."

~~~

Chapter Six: *Desperately Seeking Antichrist!* 666 Problems in Detecting the False Messiah

"Dear children, this is the last hour; and as you have heard that the antichrist is coming, even now many antichrists have come...."
~*1st John 2:18*

"Dragons coming out of the sea, Shimmering silver head of wisdom looking at me... 666 is no longer alone, he's getting out the marrow in your back bone."
~*Peter Gabriel, "Supper's Ready"*

"The antichrist" is, according to End Time authors, a false messiah and world dictator who will usher in the Tribulation and other End of the World events. For many people, the first image that comes to mind is the antichrist character Damien in the movie, *The Omen*. Damien's mother discovered a "666" birthmark or tattoo on the child's head. She was already suspicious because he fell into a frantic fit the first time the pulled up to a church. But that's Hollywood. In real life, it might be very difficult to determine Satan's spawn.

Plural Antichrists

The first of many problems with identifying the antichrist is that the Bible speaks of more than one, referring sometimes to antichrists *plural* and other times a *singular* "the antichrist." Additionally, there are different evil characters, or at least with different names, identified in the Apocalyptic writings. Lucifer, Gog, antichrist, False Prophet, serpent, dragon, beast. Although at times it would seem like these are all names identifying the exact same person, not all the various Scriptures agree on that. There are differences found in the various Bible verses regarding those various names/titles, enough to confuse us or at least to make the task of pinning down THE antichrist as a singular individual.

Only a very few New Testament verses mention antichrist(s) by that term: 1st John 2:18-22, 2nd John 1:7, and 1 John 4:2–3. Technically, the word "antichrist" only appears in the Epistles of John. But the *concept* or person we now refer to by that name is indeed referenced in many places in the Old and New Testaments.

Some Bible scholars suggest that the antichrist character is not meant to be literally a real, actual person... just an allegory or metaphor for evil coming into the world. Indeed, the Bible speaks of "the spirit of antichrist." But even if we accept that the antichrist term predicts a flesh-and-blood character, a future Hitler-type dictator, a second problem remains: the Bible's various descriptions could apply to any number of past, present or future real world leaders. The Bible describes antichrist as a "liar," which narrows the possibilities down to just 90% of all politicians and leaders who ever lived! The old joke is apt: How do you know when a politician is lying? When his lips are moving.

2nd Thessalonians 2:1-12 calls him the "lawless one." Jesus identifies the antichrist (in Matthew 24:15-16) as the same "abomination of desolation" referred to by the prophet Daniel. The Book of Revelation speaks of "the Beast," also code-numbered "666," a man of great power and a mouthpiece for "the Dragon" (Satan). (Revelation 13:11-18) The word "antichrist" is actually not found in Revelation, but the description of him is quite vivid. Unfortunately, *vivid* does not mean *helpful*; the "police sketch" one could draw from Revelation 13:2 is quite an odd creature: "And the beast which I saw was like unto a leopard, and his feet were as the feet of a bear, and his mouth as the mouth of a lion...." This just reminds us that Revelation was never intended to be taken literally. It is doubtful any of the above descriptions would help us specifically identify a real-life antichrist.

That does not stop the propheteers from jumping on even the faintest hint of an "antichrist trait" to libel any politician they dislike. Jonathan Wright, a self-styled "Bible Code-breaker," appeared on a TV talk show hosted by Rick Wiles. Together, they asserted that President Obama is the antichrist because of a housefly. On one occasion, a fly landed on Obama, and he was able to quickly catch and kill it in his hand. Rather than praise Obama's quick reflexes, they cite this as proof he is the antichrist. "[See] the flies landing on his face," Wright told Wiles, "I can show you in the [Bible] codes where he's got a strong connection to the Lord of the Flies, Beelzebub." (Beelzebub is a biblical demon who is called the "Lord of the Flies.")[19] My carport is often swarming with houseflies, so evidently the antichrist is lurking in my trashcan.

All We Have to Fear is Fear Itself

Throughout this book, I raise concerns about the negative effect that End Times sensationalism can cause. Here's another: **fear** of an antichrist could bring about a sabotage of a perfectly fine and good leader. Think about it: if a moderate, highly-effective politician arose to power in the U.S. or Europe and began to be both well-liked and successful at economic reforms and peace-building, it is likely that many evangelical Christians would grow suspicious and non-supportive. We have already seen signs of this attitude regarding the United Nations. Like any institution, the United Nations is imperfect. But UN peacekeepers have saved vast numbers of lives. UNICEF, the children's fund, has helped millions of children. These efforts have been resisted repeatedly by those Christians who view the UN as a pre-cursor to the antichrist's "one-world government."

At the extreme, more than once we've seen psychotics feed on the antichrist hype and even try to assassinate a world leader because of it. In July 2008, Jerry Blanchard, an accountant from North Carolina, made threats to kill the soon-to-be-President Obama because he believed Obama was the antichrist. In 2011, Oscar Ramiro Ortega-Hernandez attempted to assassinate the President by firing nine rounds at the White House, and he, too, felt it was his duty to "kill the antichrist." In July 1990, Gregory Stuart Gordon jumped a fence and got near former President Ronald Reagan before being stopped by Secret Service agents. He told them that Reagan was the antichrist and that "he must be killed and I must kill him." He said he had been trying to kill Reagan for 10 years. The man who shot Pope John Paul II in 1981, Turkish terrorist Mehmet Ali Agca, has hinted that he did so because of his fears about the antichrist and the end of the world. Popes now travel in bulletproof transport, the fruit of a several hundred years of rabid anti-Catholic sentiment. With its headquarters in Rome, and the Roman Empire seen as a symbol or precursor of the antichrist's future government, the Catholic Church has long been accused of being "the whore of Babylon" and thus the source for the antichrist's power.

The Number of the Beast

Few End Times writers admit it, but this 666 "beast" in Revelation is very likely a reference to Nero, the Caesar of Rome during the time the vision of Revelation was given to Saint John on the Isle of Patmos (many scholars place the writing of Revelation c.a. 90 AD, but there are strong reasons to believe the original vision was in the last year of Nero's reign). Under Rome's rule in the First Century, Christians suffered intense persecution, torture and even death. Nero scapegoated Christians for the fires that ravaged Rome in 64 AD.[20] He further alienated Christians by his extreme hubris, acting like a god. Several Roman emperors required their subjects to worship their image and to address Caesar as "Lord and God," so it made sense for St. John to project onto Rome the ancient prophecies about an earlier, evil, Babylonian leader who claimed to be god. For those and other reasons, many scholars think the true meaning of the 666 code in Revelation was a warning from John about the brutal dictator Nero the Caesar. In the Hebrew number code (*gemmatria)*, the Hebrew rendering of the name, Neron Kesar, equals 666 (incidentally, Kesar is etymologically connected to the German word for king: Kaiser). Revelation 13:18 states plainly that this was, indeed, intended as a code: "This calls for wisdom [shrewdness]. Let the person who has insight calculate [decipher] the number of the beast, for it is the number of a man. That number is 666." So, using *gemmatria*, not only does 666 match the Hebrew-spelled Neron Kesar, but the common alternate Hebrew spelling, Nero Caesar, adds up to 616, which is exactly the variant reading found in several ancient *Revelation* manuscripts for the number of the Beast. Thus, nearly all the early Catholic commentators on St. John's *Revelation* connect Nero/Caesar with the number of the Beast: as early as 2nd Century Bishop, St. Irenaeus, to St. Victorinus, Bishop of Pettau in the 3rd Century, to Commodian in the 4th and Adreaeus in the 5th.

Which Fits Best? Past or Future?

2nd Thessalonians 2:4 states, "He ...will exalt himself over everything that is called God or is worshiped, so that he sets himself up in God's temple, proclaiming himself to be God." We know that Jerusalem was sacked in AD 70 by the Roman General Titus, just two years after the death of Nero (thus the Jews may still have blamed Nero). Titus, son of Caesar, desecrated the Holy Temple in a manner predicted by Jesus' prophecy of the "abomination of desolation." This, too, likely happened during the lifetime of St. John the Revelator. And as a final connection to John's prediction that that the antichrist would die of a fatal wound but then miraculously come back to life, after Nero's suicide in 68 AD, the ancient historians Suetonius and Tacitus both reported a widespread belief Nero was not dead and would somehow return to power, or was dead and would resurrect.

Despite the fact that the best Bible scholarship points to the antichrist being a real Caesar (Nero or his kin) of St. John's time period, the propheteers are unanimous in saying he is yet to come. That fear sells more books. As we shall see, in the Seventies, the pop writers began to imagine all sorts of crazy possibilities *other* than Nero —even Ronald Wilson Reagan, because each of his names has six letters (6,6,6).

More Crying Wolf

In the "crying wolf" department, here's a partial list of more of the leaders and charismatic celebrities who have been (quite seriously) accused of being the antichrist: •Antiochus Epiphanes, the king of Syria •Pompey the Great •Caligula •Julius Caesar •a variety of Popes, including Pope John XV and Pope John Paul II (because he survived a near-fatal wound) •Charlemagne •Napoleon •Aleister Crowley •Franklin Delano Roosevelt •Benito Mussolini •Adolf Hitler •Joseph Stalin •Francisco Franco •Franklin Roosevelt •Michael Jackson •any number of heavy metal rock stars, such as KISS, Ozzy Osbourne, Marilyn Manson, etc. •King Juan Carlos of Spain •Henry Kissinger •Mikhail Gorbachev •Ayatollah Khomeini •Osama Bin Laden •Bill Clinton •several in the Bush family (see "Skull and Bones" masonic order) •Barack Obama, etc. The only thing keeping Hilary Clinton off the list is that she is a woman. We could also add a long list of self-proclaimed New Age Messiahs, starting with Sun Myung Moon, Maitreya, Louis Farrakhan, Raël, David Icke, and even rapper Kanye West.

A few more examples may be instructive in showing the absurdity of this "name the antichrist" game. Some fear John F. Kennedy would be a charismatic antichrist, because as the nation's first Roman Catholic President, he would do the

Pope's bidding (and the Catholic Church has long been accused of being a New Babylon, a New Rome, and the core of a One World government); at the 1956 Democratic convention, JFK received 666 votes; when Kennedy was shot in Dallas, some expected his head wound to heal as Revelation predicts! But my favorite example of absurdity is this candidate: Barney the Purple Dinosaur. He looks like the dragon described in Revelation; he is worshipped by children (think *Hitler Youth*); he sings of worldwide peace and love; if you play parts of his songs backwards, you can hear him say "Follow Satan." Okay, maybe no one was *truly* serious about Barney, but if you google "Barney is the antichrist" you'll get over 90,000 links!

Of all of the above names, Nero Caesar is the only one whose description fits all the references we find in Scripture. I will concede it is possible that John's words had double-meaning—applying to the Caesar of his time AND prophesying a future "Caesar-type," a One-World Government leader i.e. antichrist. But once again, the End Time propheteers are arguing against both historical/ancient scholarship and against modern mainstream scholarship.

Contradictions

As we stated, the Bible gives us very little detail about the antichrist, but even when it does, the picture can be contradictory. He can be past, present or future. He can appear attractive or monstrous. 1st Thessalonians 5:3 and Daniel 8:25 tell us that this world leader will first be a peacemaker (before later turning into a vicious warlord). This isn't much help in identifying the antichrist, because most world leaders try to first appear to be peacemakers in order to rise to power. Even Hitler, who early in his career was part of a gun-wielding coup, and invaded Poland immediately after becoming Chancellor, might still fit the definition. He was a peacemaker of sorts for a brief time during his rise in politics, as he built a coalition around the National Socialist Party. (Though Hitler matches several of the traits of an antichrist, he never invaded Jerusalem to desecrate the temple, so he could not be the one prophesied by Daniel and John.) The point here is that it would be almost impossible, using the vague descriptions in Bible prophecy, to conclusively identify "the antichrist" if such a man were to step onto the world stage.

That doesn't stop the propheteers from trying! Once they develop a pet theory, they happily discard any verse that conflicts with their "Wanted" poster that I.D.'s the antichrist. And they will adapt and apply a new theory if it at first proves wrong. After the futurists' predictions of a Russian or European antichrist lost favor (because of the decline of Russian/European power), it did not take long for them to invent a replacement candidate, a new villain *du jour*: a Muslim antichrist.

The Muslim Messiah

Most Islamic sects eagerly anticipate the coming of a messianic figure known as "the Mahdi." In Arabic, al-Mahdi means "the Guided One," also called Sahib Al-Zaman or Al-Mahdi al-Muntadhar. The revealing of this "Awaited Savior" will, supposedly, be the first in a series of signs of the Last Days. Ibn Kathir, a Muslim scholar from the 14th century, predicted, "After the lesser signs [of the end of the age] appear and increase, mankind will have reached a stage of great suffering. Then the awaited Mahdi will appear. He is the first of the greater clear signs of the Hour." One man's savior is another man's devil. In recent years, Christian End Time aficionados have begun to predict that the Islamic messiah will be Satan's antichrist. This is a radical shift from the trend of the previous 40 years, which seemed quite confident that the antichrist would be either European or Russian... a blue-eyed Aryan. Hal Lindsey, among others, pioneered the End Times scenario of a re-constituted Roman Empire, the European Union, headed by a charismatic European dictator who would one day establish a one-world government. La Haye filled in more detail, naming his fictional antichrist *Nicolae Carpathia*, a blue-eyed Romanian politician who rises to international power. In La Haye's scenario, Carpathia is named the "Sexiest Man Alive" by *People* magazine because of his charisma and magnetic personality. His popular, seductive words—at the surface friendly even to pop-Christianity—gain him control of all governments, media, and religions.

Already, La Haye's Carpathia is looking like out-dated Eurotrash, because the latest "fad" antichrist is Islamic. Two different books are now out with the exact same title: *The Islamic Antichrist*. Hal Lindsey has himself jumped on that bandwagon: his most recent end-time horror tale is about Islamic jihad.

Racial-cultural bigots get a "double-blessing" of hate by claiming that a black man, Barack Hussein Obama, is also a *Muslim* antichrist! They cite things like "Obama was raised a Muslim" and that his wedding ring is inscribed with the words (in Arabic): "No God but Allah." As for the former, while living in Indonesia as a boy, Obama attended a pseudo-Islamic school for a few years—a public primary school that is open to people of all faiths.[21] Critics fail to mention he also attended a Catholic elementary school, and for his formative High School years, a school in Hawaii that was founded by Christian missionaries. As for the ring, a clear photo close-up of it shows nothing remotely resembling Arabic calligraphy, just abstract shapes—another case of *pareidolia*.[22] If he were a "secret Muslim," it's quite a secret. He's attended Christian churches his entire adult life. And he's ticked off almost every Muslim sect there is: as Commander-in-Chief, he's ordered deadly attacks on **seven** Muslim nations, killing thousands and thousands of Muslims of all stripes—Sunni,

Shia, ISIS, etc. In January 2008, President Obama told *Christianity Today* unequivocally: "I am a Christian, and I am a devout Christian. I believe in the redemptive death and resurrection of Jesus Christ."

So which is it? Is the antichrist a white, blue-eyed European or Russian? Or a black man? Or a Muslim? The contradictory claims about the antichrist, like the other changing or conflicting theories among the propheteers, effectively disprove each other. The amazingfacts.org website states that the antichrist will come from a "kingdom somewhere in Western Europe." It insists there is "...no mistake in making this identification." "Don't forget all these identification points come directly from the Bible. They are not some human opinion or speculation." So, there you have it, according to that website, the Bible insists the antichrist is European. Not Muslim.

Obama is neither.

The Islamic Scenario "Proves" the End is Not Near

For those who insist upon a literal view of Bible prophecy, Joel Richardson convincingly argues that the antichrist will be a Muslim. (I am not saying I agree with his conclusions, but rather, I am again using the literalists' own contradictions to expose their fallacy.) In his recent book, *The Islamic Antichrist: The Shocking Truth about the Real Nature of the Beast*, Richardson correctly points out that the Bible (the books of Daniel and Revelation in particular) **speaks of the antichrist as a *religious* leader**, leading a movement that most of the world will embrace as its "world faith." This rules out Russia and China, since they are ideologically and officially *secularist* governments, and they are, in practice, more "anti-Muslim" than even Israel (in the modern era, Russia has killed more Muslims than Israel has). Herein lies a problem for Richardson's Islamic scenario: it's hard to imagine world domination that includes both a theocracy *and* agnostic countries like Russia and China. Quoting Richardson at length: "[T]he Antichrist and his 'beast kingdom,' [shall be] a powerful empire with an equally powerful military machine. Daniel the Prophet describes this empire and its military as a force 'terrifying and frightening and very powerful' that 'will devour the whole earth.' ...The fourth beast is a fourth kingdom that will appear on earth. It ...will devour the whole earth, trampling it down and crushing it. Thus the Bible gives us a clear picture... of Satan's coming empire, the goal of which will be nothing less than total world domination. [It will demand] total submission to and worship of its leader, the Antichrist...."

The contradiction is obvious: How will, anytime in the next twenty years, a religious/Islamic leader at once make Islam the world religion AND conquer the world militarily, when the U.S., Russia, China and Israel are all adamantly opposed to Islamic rule? The Top Nine strongest militaries on the globe belong to non-Muslim countries. By contrast, combine the militaries of Turkey, Saudi Arabia, Pakistan, Iran, Iraq, Egypt, Syria, and any other Muslim country of your choosing. They would not come close to equaling the air and naval power of the United States alone. The tiny country of Israel has a stronger Air Force than all other Middle Eastern countries *combined.* You cannot conquer the world without a global Navy and Air Force. The "Muslim antichrist" has no hope of assembling either.

[Let me add a note here: I am **not** labeling Joel Richardson a "propheteer." He stands apart from the other authors I've criticized herein: he does not pretend to know specific dates for the End Times, he writes intelligently about Scripture and understands metaphor, and seems to be a person of grace, not judgment.]

More Fearmongering Debunked

When assessing the "Muslim threat," consider that half of

the Islamic countries have major civil unrest and divisive factions within their own lands, add in the hatred between Sunni and Shia sects and nationalistic animosities, and the result is a zero chance of their forming a harmonious, united Islamic army powerful enough to "totally dominate" the world. Even with a shared hatred of Israel by a dozen Middle Eastern countries, those Islamic countries have come nowhere near "dominating" the Middle East, much less the whole world. It would take twenty years for those political realities to change, and during those two decades, you can bet neither communists nor capitalists are going to sit back and let it happen.

Some fearmongers have spun tales of a Muslim "takeover" of the U.S. from inside, via immigration, high Muslim birth rates, and then the imposition of "Sharia Law." Fact: Sharia Law has never been instituted in *any* city in the United States; less than 1% of the U.S. population is Muslim, and that tiny minority is divided into competing sects. Some conservative websites trumpeted the fearmongering headline: **Dearborn, Michigan Becomes First U.S. City to Implement Sharia Law**. Turns out it was from a satire site... a joke! It never happened. Even if it did happen, it would not stand up in court, because Sharia Laws would violate our Constitution. And it would take a two-thirds vote of Congress to change that, thanks to our Constitution's church and state clause. The *Pew Forum on Religion and Public Life* projects that the Muslim population in the U.S. will grow by only **1.7%** by 2030. Gee, less than 2% of our population... I'm trembling in my boots.

So there are serious problems with fully matching a world-dominating antrichrist with any scenario: Muslim, European, Russian or Chinese. The literal view of Bible prophecy, if it is honest to its own methods and thorough in including *all* pertinent verses, cannot explain how all the conflicting conditions of Daniel and Revelation can be fulfilled within a single antichrist in our times. And the contradictions of our current political reality cannot be overcome in my lifetime.

Every propheteer's scenario of the last two hundred years has been wrong, and now the latest notion to "blame the Muslims" is self-contradictory. Will the purveyors of End Times pulp fiction ever quit?

~~~

Chapter Seven: *Pot Calling Kettle, Pot Calling Kettle* False Prophets, False Profits, and True Hypocrisy

"Beware of false prophets, who come to you in sheep's clothing, but inwardly they are ravenous wolves."
   ~*Matthew 7:15*

"Woe to you, teachers of the law and Pharisees, you hypocrites! You clean the outside of the cup and dish, but inside they are full of greed and self-indulgence."
   ~*Matthew 23:25*

   The propheteers worry about the arrival of a false prophet (the sidekick to the antichrist)... but are they false prophets themselves? The Scripture above makes it clear that the biblical test for a false prophet is a simple one. A true prophet will not repeatedly make predictions that prove to be false. The Church has been greatly discredited by "false prophets," pastors and authors who make sensationalistic claims that the world is going to end "next year," or the Great Tribulation and Rapture is coming "soon."

If Raptured, Can I Take My Retirement Account Along?
   The "Left Behind" series of books are in the Top Five of ALL TIME in book series... up there with *Harry Potter* or *The Lord of the Rings.* While ostensibly a work of fiction, its predictions of political events are essentially the same as what Tim LaHaye also forecasts in his non-fictional book, *Are We Living in the End Times?* That 2011 book was put together using materials dated a few years prior. Now, as we move into 2015, we find that nothing has happened as LaHaye predicted. Actually, if you survey all of LaHaye's writings, he has had us poised on the brink of the "Last Days" for some 20 years now. This raises the question: *If these guys truly believe the Second Coming is imminent, why do they have nice, fat savings and retirement accounts?*

Of course, I'm not just picking on LaHaye. A hundred more "End Times" authors are out there, and most of their ideas were voiced some 50 years earlier by Hal Lindsey. He wrote *The Late Great Planet Earth* in 1969... a premature obituary for our planet. Lindsey's seminal work was one of the best-selling books throughout the Seventies. Almost everything he predicted turned out to be wrong. One specific and huge mistake: in 1970 he predicted that Christ's visible return would occur "within forty years or so of 1948," that is, by 1988. (1948 marked the reforming of the Jewish nation in Israel.) Who knew that "or so" could mean being off by another quarter-century... or so. Undaunted when his 1970 predictions failed, Lindsay re-released his books in variously-updated versions again and again, one each few years, including *Planet Earth 2000 A.D.: Will Mankind Survive?*, published in 1996. Hal, you would be wise not to put dates on your book covers, it shortens their marketable shelf life! Twenty years after he wrote that updated eulogy for the world (i.e. around 2000 AD), most of us are "still alive and well" (though ironically, Johnny Winter, who wrote the song, "Still Alive and Well," is not).

Rogue's Gallery

What follows in this chapter is a "Hall of Shame" gallery of the obscene extremes of wealth and greed amongst the celebrity "Christian" writers, TV evangelists and megachurch pastors. (And not all of these have exploited Rapture hysteria for money, but most on this list are sympathetic with the "Jesus is coming tomorrow" mindset.)

Rev. John Hagee's books have made him millions—and he pulled in a TV-evangelist's inflated salary even as he wrote them. He has a congregation of over 20,000. He reaches far, far more with his books, in which he arrogantly claims absolute knowledge of God's intent. Because his predictions are more recent than some of his ilk, time has not yet disproven everything Hagee has claimed, but already we've seen that his crystal ball is fractured. Hypocritically, he is quick to accuse others of being "false prophets." In his book on End Time prophecy, *Four Blood Moons*, Hagee wrote: "Any person presenting the gospel of Jesus Christ who does not teach or preach the literal Word of God is a false prophet." That is actually **not** what the Bible says (in fact, Jesus taught chiefly in parables, which are metaphorical, not "literal." Literally. Instead, the Bible offers **guidance on how to expose a false prophet:**

•**If their predictions prove false.** Deuteronomy 18:22: "If what a prophet proclaims in the name of the LORD does not take place or come true, that is a message the LORD has not spoken. That prophet has spoken presumptuously...."

•**If they are motivated mostly by money.** Jesus warned of false teachers "full of greed and self-indulgence" (Matthew 23:25) who "devour widows' houses" (Mark 12:40).

Hagee fails both of these tests. The John Hagee "Rabbi Trust" includes a $2.1 million 7,969-acre ranch with five lodges, plus a manager's house, a smokehouse, a skeet range, three large barns, and an airport. Hagee's personal payment package is one of the highest of any non-profit director in Texas.[23]

For all the multi-millions these authors/pastors have made, can we point to any significant value they have brought the Kingdom of God on earth by these books? Remember, many of them have "ministries" that are funded separately by tithes and donations of parishioners. Where do those insane riches go? Into private bank accounts, mansions, car collections, jet planes and lavish living.[24] Even if Hagee were sincere and accurate in his End Times teachings, I would still call him a fraud for this simple reason: he professes to be preaching the Truth of Jesus Christ, but his multi-million-dollar lifestyle is a direct repudiation of Jesus' teachings on love, caring and sharing. Jesus warned that the rich man (called *Dives* in the Latin) who reclined in luxury whilst he ignored the paralyzed beggar at his doorstep would burn in Hades. From what little the parable tells us, Hagee's lifestyle far exceeds that of the biblical rich man, who was "in agony because of the flames."

In event of Rapture, may I have your Mercedes?

A most obvious sign of a false prophet is the dollar $ign. When we see greed and lavish living by those associated with the End Times movement, it points to a nefarious "motive" in the same way that a husband standing over the body of a dead wife is considered a greater suspect if he has her five million dollar life insurance policy in his hand. On the surface, these writers are showy with their passion for Christ's return, but when we dig deeper, we find that something else is motivating them—sales of books and DVD's—and we also find they are ensconced in luxury, contradicting their own urgent cry to "get ready!"

But many of this ilk are masters at hiding their wealth, at downplaying the degree to which they live more like Caligula or Donald Trump than they do like Jesus the Suffering Servant. Most of the very wealthiest evangelists (Pat Robertson, Hagee, Osteen, Meyer, etc.) set up trusts and annuities so that assets are no longer purely in their name. Many put their spouses or family members into cushy, high-paying jobs or free "parsonages," as Joyce Meyer and Joel Osteen both did with their multiple nespotic hirings. And most have access to transportation paid for by their ministries—including chauffeurs and private jets. The church bulletin for the Crystal Cathedral once ran a request for casseroles to be given to Robert Schuller's wife during her homebound illness. The article informed parishioners to drop dishes off at the church office—where the Schuller's chauffeur would pick up the free food and deliver it to their mansion in the limo! As one country song put it, if Jesus were physically walking the earth today, would he "wear a Rolex on his television show?"

Treasure Hidden in Plain Sight

The best cover for lavish living is to make a celebrity-pastor's working environment into a paradise of luxury: the indulgence can thus be enjoyed without cost, without taxation and without the parishioners counting it as part of the pastors' compensation. Trinity Broadcast Networks HQ is a perfect example of such a workplace palace: a 65,000 square-foot building that houses a TV studio, bookstore and theater, plus a finely-appointed suite of offices for TBN founder **Paul Crouch**. The lobby wows visitors with its baroque marble staircase and 15-foot-high statue of Archangel Michael guarding 217 hand-painted cherubs on the lobby ceiling... the total cost of everything: over $8.5 million. Oh, lest you think I've forgotten our topic: another impressively-painted mural at TBN depicts Jesus riding a white stallion, flanked by three warrior angels, in an equestrian depiction of the Second Coming.

Of course, TBN's palace pales in comparison to Joel Osteen's gigantic Lakewood church, arena and office complex, where the renovations alone cost $95 million, according to a 2005 article in *USA Today*.

Joel and Victoria Osteen live in a ten-million-dollar mansion with six bathrooms, three elevators and a pool house. But the estate is technically owned by "Covenant Trust," so the Osteens can claim they don't own it. It's not clear who pays the $200,000 annual property tax on it.

Perhaps Pastor **Kenneth Copeland** is "homeless," since he also lives in a parsonage he (technically) doesn't own. The mansion-parsonage is owned by Kenneth Copeland Ministries, and it is a far cry from the gospel message of "do not store up treasure on earth." The Copeland mansion is a huge $6 million lakehouse on 25 acres—all with tax-exempt status. This man's castle boasts doors that came from a real castle, plus a grand spiral staircase and bridge that spans across the living room and connects the two sides of the house, but still leaves room for huge crystal chandeliers. Six garages shelter the Copeland's motorcycles, cars and golf cart, but that's not their only vehicle storage area: a boat dock with three slips usually is filled with boats, but if the weather is bad, they can always tuck the boats safely in the nearby airplane hangars! That's right, hanga*r*s, plural. As of 2010, Copeland Ministries kept nine aircraft based at their private airport: four single-engine, three multi-engine, and two jet-engine airplanes.[25]

    The aptly-named **Creflo Dollar**, a friend of Copeland's, borrowed his prosperity message and used it to create his own prosperity that rival's Copeland's. Mr. Dollar drives a Rolls Royce, flies in a private jet between his million-dollar residences in Atlanta and a $2.5 million apartment in Manhattan. He enjoys the best of everything… literally living better than kings. I bet he's in no hurry for the end of time to come.

    Joyce Meyer is one TV-evangelist who might seem at first glance to be less guilty of the excessive lifestyle… she comes across on TV as a simple, unpretentious housewife. But again, like many of her cohorts, she minimizes the amount of possessions in her *name*, yet still available for her use: she has established the lavishly-furnished Joyce Meyer Ministry Headquarters (with its $23,000 marble-topped commode/cabinet and $11,219 French clock), an associated Family Compound, an Irrevocable Trust, and fat salaries spread out amongst her kin… so she can claim to not be a multi-millionaire even though the Meyers live like they are. At one point, Joyce and her family each enjoyed top-of-the-line Lexus automobiles, except for Meyer's husband: he drove a Mercedes-Benz S55 AMG sedan. But luxury cars are nothing compared to the cost of the ministry's Gulfstream G-

IV jet, with its two full-time pilots, ready to fly the globe-trotting Meyers on a moment's notice. Of course, none of this is in her name (which means she pays no taxes on any of it nor does she personally have to pay the maintenance costs). The accoutrements that surround Joyce Meyer are more luxuriant than those found in Wall Street offices: over $50,000 worth of European vases and porcelain, two $5,800 curio cabinets (one HAS to have a place to put all the ceramics and crystal), a $5,700 porcelain of the Crucifixion, a $30,000 malachite round table … this partial list is just the tip of the iceberg of literally millions spent on furnishings there. The ministry has also provided five mansions: one for Joyce and for each of her four children. We don't have space here to detail the Meyers' golf putting range, swimming pools, guest house, vacation home, boat, jet ski, etc. She says she won't "apologize for God's blessings." She's been especially blessed with the laws on Irrevocable Trusts and the Bill of Rights' separation of church and state, which protect her from taxation on most of her Midas lifestyle.

"Bishop" **T.D. Jakes** also talks a good game about personal humility. But his $2.6 million luxurious seven-bedroom home and indoor swimming pool in the affluent White Rock Lake area of Dallas, says differently.

Benny Hinn, on the other hand, has no pretense of humility regarding his lifestyle. One look at Hinn's Liberace-level wardrobe and jewelry should be a clue where he puts his heart and treasure… yet thousands of people still donate to his "ministry," funding his $10 million seaside mansion, a private jet, a Mercedes SUV and convertible, lavish shopping, and his traveling "crusades" that include vacation-like layovers between each event at the cost of $900 - $3,000 per *night* in the best suites of resort hotels in Hawaii, Cancun, London, Milan, etc. No wonder the watchdog organization, *Ministry Watch*, added Benny Hinn Ministries to its naughty list of "Donor Alerts." Personally, any church or ministry entitled "My Name Ministries" instead of "Jesus Christ Ministries" gives me pause.

Speaking of which, there's **John Hagee** Ministries. Hagee is the founder and Senior Pastor of Cornerstone Church in Texas, with some 20,000 members. He is also President of John Hagee Ministries and its international media empire (Global Evangelism Television), broadcasting his message on prosperity-via-faith, plus End Times fear-mongering… two philosophies that seem at odds with each other. Of course, Hagee draws a paycheck from all the various pies he has his fingers in, including a small fortune from books and DVD's… and for good measure, his wife draws a couple of fat paychecks as well. We've elsewhere mentioned how he protects much of his wealth by parking it in "The John Hagee Rabbi Trust." Taken together, the Hagee family income and assets make Jed Clampett and Granny look like hillbilly paupers.

LaHaye and Left Behind

Before we leave this topic, we have to revisit Tim LaHaye's money-making machine. The human mind is not very good at grasping very large numbers. We can't really appreciate how huge a number like a "million" is, because we rarely ever count beyond a hundred. So when I tell you that LaHaye has sold millions of End Times books, you probably don't fully appreciate the size and scope of it. At one time, his series titles filled four of five slots in the *New York Times* Top 5 bestsellers' list (not just "religious books"). His tenth title in the series is still going strong. You'd think after nine books, people would lose interest, but that tenth volume hit Number One. Over fifty million books bearing the logo of the "Left Behind" series have flowed through both Christian and secular bookstores, but that's only half the iceberg. LaHaye's fourteen novels are accompanied by a mega-multi-media franchise: several motion pictures, over twenty children's books, several study guides, many non-fiction books on prophecy, plus books with his wife on other topics, like marriage and politics.

Tim LaHaye was born in 1926, fought in World War II and after the war, attended Bob Jones University. Bob Jones U is a fundamentalist school known for intense anti-Catholicism and racism (it did not accept African-American students until the 1970's, and until 2000, had a student-body policy against interracial dating). LaHaye met his wife, Beverly, there, and together they have shared his ministry both in churches and in writing. They have also have been very active in Rightwing Republican politics together. Tim was a co-founder of Jerry Falwell's *Moral Majority*, and Beverly founded *Concerned Women for America*, a large organization of conservative Christian women that stands as a polar opposite to the *National Organization for Women (NOW)*. In 1987, Tim became co-chair of Senator Jack Kemp's presidential campaign. So the LaHaye's not only have a great fortune, they have great power and influence.

Money, Power and Influence by the End Times Gang

The LaHayes are not alone in this partnership between politicians and propheteers. Other politicians hold similar views about the End Time and/or are influenced by the End Time writers. We have already cited Hal Lindsey's connection with high-placed Pentagon officials. John Hagee was closely associated with John McCain's presidential campaign. Michele Bachmann was until recently a prominent member of Congress. She takes too much glee in the prospect of a World War Three Armageddon. "We get to be living in the most exciting time in history," she said, urging Christians to "rejoice." "Jesus Christ is coming back. We, in our lifetimes potentially, could see Jesus Christ returning to Earth, the Rapture of the Church. We need to realize how close this clock is to getting towards the midnight hour,"

Bachmann concluded. Ronald Reagan shared with friends that he thought he was part of God's plan to bring about the End of Days. Thankfully, he never drove us over the brink into a World War... but had Gorbachev been as hawkish as Reagan, would the Cold War have escalated into nuclear war?

LaHaye's co-author, Jerry B. Jenkins, has published several dozen books of his own, too. If you took all the products that the LaHayes and Jenkins have produced, you could fill the entire "Religion and Spirituality" section of a Barnes & Nobles (but the substantive content could be reduced to a single issue of *Reader's Digest*). Jenkins and LaHaye are proud of the numbers; they like to claim they are leading souls to Christ via their books. But how many are they driving *away* from Christ by their flagging credibility?

One Rotten Apple Spoiling the Bunch?

Now let me clarify: I am NOT saying all End Time authors and pastors are greedy. For example, this book cites Perry Stone's false prophecies, but I don't think he abuses his wealth in the vulgar, outsized manner of many of his colleagues. But there is no doubt in my mind that many of those obsessed with the idea of an immediate Second Coming have blinders on about their own sin of greed—which seems rather ironic. If they truly believe Jesus is coming back in a few months, why have they spent so much time and energy building earthly palaces? Joyce Meyer, in response to a critic of her ministry's extravagance, defended it by saying these were great "investments" for her church. Real estate may indeed be a good investment, but all experts would tell you it is a *long-term* investment, thus a rather strange choice if one really believes that time is about to expire.

This book is not intended as a comprehensive study of greedy, ego-obsessed evangelists. If it were, our list could, sadly, go on: "Bishop" Elijah Bernard Jordan (his multi-million dollar mansion features a large painting of Jordan on a throne with his three sons around him as angels), Pat Robertson (mountaintop mansion with an airstrip, diamond and gold mines in Africa, and a media empire), Paula and Randy White ($2.1 million mansion and a $3.5 million Trump Tower condo, before they divorced), Fred Price, Juanita Bynum ($4.5 million estate and jewelry fit for royalty), Mike Murdock (uses a $4,500 fountain pen), Robert Tilton, a modern version of a snake-oil salesman who threw hundreds of unread prayer requests in the dumpster after extracting the donation checks that fund his mansions and 50-foot yacht, *et cetera ad nauseum*. The point here is that the false prophets are revealed not only by their false **prophecies**, but also by their sinful **profits**… diverting tithes and offerings into their own pockets that should have gone to help the needy and to spread the real gospel in a physically and spiritually- hungry Third World.

Jesus said, "Watch out for false prophets…. By their fruit you will recognize them." (Matthew 7:15-16)

~~~

Chapter Eight: *Two Sides of the Same Coin:* Christian and Islamic Apocalypticism

"But I say to you, Love your enemies and pray for those who persecute you."
~Jesus in Matthew 5:44

"Love is made complete among us so that we will have confidence on the day of judgment.... [But] whoever does not love their brother and sister... cannot love God."
~1st John 4:17 and 20, excerpted

If you find yourself looking in the mirror and seeing a face that looks all too much like your mortal enemy (supposedly your polar opposite), it might be time to have a deeper look. Read some Carl Jung on the topic of the Shadow and the *Doppelgänger*. Often the darkness we fear is but a shadow-twin of our own worse traits.

Extremist Muslims and Extremist Christians do indeed share all too many commonalities, including a mutual cockiness in their claims of foresight about Armageddon. As we look to the overlap in their eschatologies, first consider this chart:

Fundamentalist Islam	**Fundamentalist Christian**
Uses Scripture as ultimate authority	Scripture / Holy Spirit
Interprets Scripture literally	Yes, down to the letter
Divine revelation set in concrete	God's Word unchanging
Hostile to science	Suspicious of science
Hates modern Western culture	Condemns modernity
Emphasizes law, wrath, retribution	Ditto

And both sides share:
An obsession with sexual purity and vehement homophobia
Male-dominated leadership (with few exceptions)

Urge subservience in women
Dichromatic view of the world: believers vs. heretics/pagans
Both expect Jesus soon to wage war in the Apocalypse
Both expect a False Prophet and antichrist who will kill Jews
Both expect that the End Times will arrive any day now
Both accuse the other of being Satanic.
~~

Who is The Great Satan?

In most End of the World books of the Seventies, the USSR was the boogeyman... after *glasnost* and the break-up of the Soviet Union, suddenly the same prophecies no longer seemed to apply to Russia, they focused more on the rising dragon of China... and then in recent years, a new villain, Islam... and so, amazingly (ha), the same prophecies that once matched Russia and China now perfectly fit the Muslim countries instead.

In yet another irony, some of these writers are beginning to see their own country, the United States, as the agent of the antichrist who will fulfill the horrible role of a war on Israel... the irony being that the Muslim countries have been trying to tell us all along that we are The Great Satan.

This isn't really funny. The sad paradox is that many of the "Christian" fundamentalists have more in common with the Taliban than with moderate, orthodox Christianity. Radical Islam and Extreme-fundamentalist Christianity share a world-view that includes: male dominance over women; persecution of homosexuals; unthinking legalistic view of scriptures; sexual repression; judgmentalism; eager endorsement of "holy war;" disdain for academic education; an embrace of gross wealth inequality. Yet they hate each other, as Dr. Carl Jung could have predicted, and are unable to see they are mirror image *doppelgängers*.

True Believers vs. True Believers

I am not the first person to take note of the striking similarities between conservative Christian eschatologists and conservative Islamic eschatologists. In a well-researched article for *The Atlantic* magazine, Graeme Wood writes of ISIS, the so-called "Islamic State," that "the End of Days is a leitmotif of its propaganda."[26] As the Iraq war unfolded, Islamic extremists "saw signs of the end times everywhere. They were anticipating [soon] the arrival of the Mahdi—a messianic figure destined to lead the Muslims to victory before the end of the world." ISIS believes in the prophecies of a final battle of Armageddon on the plains of Dabiq; Christians prophesy the battle will be on the plains of Megiddo... just a few hundred miles apart.

"True believers" may point to these similarities as confirmation of End Times prophecy, but how do they reconcile that both groups see each other in opposite roles of good vs. evil? Rather than both being right, or one being right and one being wrong, history tells us it is far more likely that **both are wrong**, both extremes driven by a psychological need to believe the time in which they live is especially significant and dramatic.

Blood Brothers

Christian and Muslim fundamentalists share a frightening philosophy: they see nothing much wrong with spilling blood if it is for a "good cause." Based on how both extremes portray the End of Time battles of Armageddon, we can only conclude that both sides actually believe war is *good*, because it achieves God's eschatological plan. They both are eager to rush in where angels fear to tread... into a violent and bloody holy war (what a tragic oxymoron: "bloody holy war"). When each side calls the other Satanic, there is no room for compromise. And when each side blindly and self-righteously follows their literalistic views of Scripture, but *different* Scriptures, there is no room for the humility required to acknowledge the ambiguity inherent in all ancient texts. They are like two identical freight trains, heading down the same track, but unfortunately headed for a collision.

Fifty Shades of Grey in Black and White

What fuels these two locomotives, steaming out of control? Words. Words drive both sides of these religious and cultural passions. But unfortunately, they fail to look for the Spirit beneath the words.

Language (whether it be Hebrew or Arabic) is by its nature ambiguous. Fundamentalists seek for black and white answers, but language is in shades of grey. Words have multiple shades of meanings, and only the original writer knows for sure what palette he intended. The narrative context is, of course, a huge clue, as is the cultural point in history and even the geography. One of my favorite examples was related as a first-hand experience by a Catholic priest from England when he was lecturing an American audience. He told a story in which he had visited a colleague, a nun. He said, "I went and knocked her up." In his English parlance, that simply meant he knocked on the nun's door. The American audience, however, burst into laughter because in the U.S. context, "knocked up" means sex or even impregnation! So when we cherry-pick a verse and quote it as a stand-alone premise, without understanding its original context, we often arrive at ridiculous conclusions about meaning.

To My Christian Brothers and Sisters

As a Christian, I doubt my words will be heard by many Muslim readers. So these words are particularly for my Christian brothers and sisters: I view the Old Testament through a New Testament lens. I write as a passionate believer, but also as an educated pastor, and with an understanding of Judaic history. The harsh laws of the Old

Testament were in the context of a barbaric time in Jewish history, where the countries surrounding them were barbaric, and in many cases the Israelites themselves were barely one step above barbarism. Jesus brought an entirely new era of religious understanding and instituted a new relationship with God. He fulfilled the Old Testament laws and offered a new connection to a God of mercy, grace and love. His New Covenant was about pardon and redemption, and Jesus said, "If anyone hears my words but does not keep them, I do not judge that person. For I did not come to judge the world, but to save the world." (John 12:47) For some reason (perhaps because a literalistic view of Scripture is a pre-requisite for modern eschatology), **the majority of End Times authors ignores this New Testament view** and revert to a wrathful God of the Old Covenant, a God who seems more intent on punishing people than on redeeming them. Again, Hagee is one of my "favorite" examples. He wrote (in *Blood Moons*): "And just as Hitler planned a 'Final Solution' [genocide] for the Jewish people, God is planning a final solution for the *enemies* of Israel... God will kill 84 percent of the [pagan] army" that invades Israel. "By stoning," Hagee happily adds. He is literally saying God will be as harshly cruel to pagans "just as Hitler" was to the Jews. *Wow*, so much for the words of Jesus who said, "And I, when I am lifted up from the earth, will draw all people to myself." (John 12:32) All people. Not just an elect few.

Racial Myth

This is where the fundamentalists part ways. Some of the worst extremes of Christian fundamentalism cling to a racial myth of white Aryan-supremacy that would exclude the darker skins of Middle Eastern Muslims (and ironically, the dark skin of Jesus, too). I suspect that the fundamentalists' hatred of Islam has more to do with their racist attitude about skin color than with religious differences. The virulent anti-immigration movement in the U.S., which explicitly states its desire to "protect the values of white Anglo-Celtic culture," runs tandem with the same demographic of John Hagee's congregation. Hagee preached to his mostly-white congregation in San Antonio that people "on welfare" are "lazy" and should get their "nasty self off the couch and go get a job." A racial component was implied but clear when we remember he spoke in an area with a high Hispanic population, as he bemoaned a welfare population that could constitute, he added, "a dependent state the size of Spain."[27]

Hagee's ideology is in the same stream as the 19th-20th century "Christian Identity Movement," which taught that whites are the true descendants of the biblical Israelites, and identified the United States and/or the British isles as the "true" descendants of the Ten Lost Tribes of Israel. The racial purity desired by that brand of "Christianity" is in direct opposition to the teachings of Jesus, who lifted up the racially-outcast Samaritan as a better neighbor than the racially-pure priest.

Through the Looking Glass: Mirrored Fear

Both Muslim and Christian extremists are bound to their extremism by the common tie of *fear*. Both extremes tend to be at the margins of socioeconomic classes. The dispossessed find something strangely empowering about the prospect of ending the present social order, even if by apocalyptic flames. They hope God will swoop in with a "grapes of wrath" vengeance upon their enemies, so then they can surf on waves of blood to land on the beaches of the Promised Land. It is a twisted hope, but a hope nonetheless, and hope is a commonly-employed remedy for fear and powerlessness. Despite sharing the same self-righteous, harsh, legalistic moralism, these two sides each fear the "otherness" of a culture and people who are, ironically, very different in exterior lifestyles whilst rooted in twin longings for vengeance.

That fear is understandable, as it stems from a violent "us and them" reality: almost every Middle Easterner has experienced *us* in a negative way, as the United States (sometimes via our proxy, Israel), has either bombed, shot-up or exploited the people and resources (oil) of their countries. And *they* (Muslims) are "famous" to us as either Ottoman invaders of white Europe or suicide-bombing terrorists. Yet, in cold, numerical objective measures, modern Islamic extremists are less of a threat to the average American than lightning and snakebites, and in turn, the average Middle Eastern Muslim has suffered more at the hands of fellow Arabic leaders than from us: the greed and oppression of Saddam Hussein, Muammar Gaddafi, the Saudi kings, Hosni Mubarak, and their ilk has harmed Muslims more than Chevron oil ever did. (To speak of "average," I'm referring to those not directly affected by abnormal events—the wars in Iraq and Afghanistan and the 9-11 attacks— which obviously are more serious for their victims than snakebites.)

Peace and Love

The vast majority of Americans and the vast majority of Muslims just want to live their lives in peace. It is my strong faith belief that the answer is found not in a vengeful God, but in a loving God. I am a Christian, but I cannot accept the Rightwing theology of Christian fundamentalism. I also totally reject the flawed foundations of fundamentalist Islam. I don't have any dislike of, or ill will toward, Baptist or Muslim individuals. I commend to both extremes these verses from what is one of the greatest chapters in Scripture— **1st John 4:** "Dear friends, do not believe every spirit, but test the spirits to see whether they are from God, because many false prophets have gone out into the world.... Dear friends, let us love one another, for love comes from God.... Whoever does not love does not know God, because God is love.... This is how love is made complete among us so that we will have confidence on the day of judgment: In this world we are like Jesus. There is no fear in love. But perfect love drives out fear, because fear has to do with punishment. The one who fears is not made perfect in love.... Anyone who loves God must also love their brother and sister."

Mirror Opposites... or Brothers?

Both the Bible and the Qur'an teach that Isaac (father of Israelis) is the brother of Ishmael (father of Arabs). Thus the following Sufi wisdom (from the Islamic mystic, Rūmī) applies to both "brothers": "If you find fault in your brother or sister, the fault you see in them is within yourself. The true Sufi is like a mirror where you see your own image, for 'The believer is a mirror of their fellow believers.' Get rid of those faults in yourself, because what bothers you in them bothers you in yourself."

Perhaps rather than crediting C. G. Jung, I should credit Muhammad Rūmī, who taught that dualities like "us vs. them" are illusions, which vanish when we realize our enemy is merely our twin, and when we embrace God above Self. Rūmī added, "The seeker of truth is a mirror for their neighbors. But those who cannot feel the sting of truth are not mirrors to anyone...."

~~~

Chapter Nine: *Deep and Wide*
A Deeper, More Thorough Study of Meaning

"Above all, you must understand that no prophecy of Scripture came about by the prophet's own interpretation of things. For prophecy never had its origin in the human will."
~*2nd Peter 1:20-21*

"Jesus replied, 'You are in error because you do not know the Scriptures or the power of God.'"
~*Matthew 22:29*

   Does the reader now think that I merely scoff at Scriptures regarding the Apocalypse? To the contrary, not only do I take all Scripture seriously, I also believe that eschatology and apocalyptic Scriptures have deeper meaning, ignored by the "pop" exploitational books. Let us look deeper: deeper into how we read, study and understand the Bible, and deeper into the mystical, visionary images found in Ezekiel, Daniel, and St. John's writing.

Anti-Academics
   TV preachers and End Times authors are very loud in proclaiming their love of the Bible... and quick to condemn those with an academic understanding that challenges their view. The propheteers are quick to label intellectuals as unspiritual "liberals." I'll not join a contest as to which person has spiritual superiority, but I truly love God and firmly believe my respect for Scripture is as dedicated as anyone's. And at the risk of being judgmental, I must say that many of these authors employ Scripture in a disrespectful manner (manipulating Scripture rather than submitting to it). They approach Bible study in a narrow and shallow way, and they somehow view their own tunnel-vision faith as a virtue. It is not. Jesus and Paul were both Bible scholars (in their case, the Jewish "Bible"), and both encouraged followers to

dig deep for meaning. As Paul put it, we are to "no longer be infants," but should "become mature" by growing "in the knowledge of the Son of God," reaching "the whole measure of the fullness of Christ" (Ephesians 4:13-14)

As a kid in Vacation Bible School, we learned a song about God's grace entitled, "Deep and Wide." This could be applied to Bible verses, too: we should **dig deep and wide to understand "the whole measure of the fullness" of God's message.**

We don't have to look far to find examples of half-measured Bible study. A guest Op-Ed writer in the *Birmingham News* (February 23, 2015), wrote: "If you have a scripture verse you have an answer, everything else is an opinion." But he then proceeded to pour *his* opinion on us, to pick *which* verses to use and *how* to interpret them. This Bible literalist, citing "God's inflexible and righteous judgment," harshly condemned anyone with a different view of Scripture. He seemed oblivious to the fact that the Bible is rich, complex and nuanced... and that most verses have more than one meaning. Such narrow-mindedness rejects the fact that across 2,000 years of Christendom, each Bible verse has had different interpretations and emphases. For example, would the op-ed writer be as literal about obeying Exodus 35:2, which plainly states: "Whoever does any work on [the Sabbath] must be put to death." If a literalist has so much as flipped a pancake on a Sabbath, that is **work** (according to Hebrew tradition), and thus he must be put to death for it... that is, if going by the reasoning of, "If you have a Scripture verse you have an answer." I find it frustrating when reasonably-intelligent people can't see the logical fallacy of literalism.

Misapplication: Prophecies that Apply to That, not This

So returning to our topic, we find ample examples of End Time writers misapplying Scripture. Mark Biltz cites an upsurge of interest in the Hebrew language that, he says, began in the early 1900's and continues now in these "Last Days." He sees this as a fulfillment of a prophecy in Zephaniah 3:9, where, according to Biltz, the Lord will "turn to the people a pure language...." Not "return" but "turn." The original word here is (literally) more akin to flipping a pancake—turning up a different, fresh side. And the word "language," in verse 3:9, is better translated as "speech." So the intent of this verse is that Zephaniah is predicting a time of a fresh start, when people's speech will be renewed and made pure/holy. The passage makes no reference whatsoever to the Hebrew language, nor to a future time when Hebrew would "make a comeback," as Biltz projects.

Let's look at more examples of similar misapplication, this time in Ezekiel 28-29. In End Time books, misapplication is often driven by a bias, the belief that the United States is God's *other* Chosen Nation, a twin to Israel, and in such a world view, our enemies must be the ones that Ezekiel was alluding to. Let's ignore, for the moment, the narcissism implicit in believing that the bulk of Bible prophecy was written about *our* nation and *our* time. Instead, let's stick to Bible study.

Before Islamic extremists became the predominant threat in the mind of many Christian fundamentalists, Hal Lindsey and most other End Time writers of the Seventies and early Eighties figured that surely our big, scary, godless enemies—Russia and China—would be the main players in the End of Time final battle. So they became convinced that Gog and Magog stand for Russia and the "Kings of the East" refers to China. Indeed, Lindsey dedicated a chapter to each (in *The Late, Great Planet Earth*): one entitled "Russia is a Gog" and another with the politically-incorrect title, "The Yellow Peril" (China). In some Bible references, Gog is a man, an evil ruler, and other times, a place or country. Geographic specifics are scant: Ezekiel refers to Magog as a country in the "uttermost north," but one could flip a coin on whether this is Turkey/Asia Minor or Russia, as both are due north of Israel. **Through the eyes of an ancient prophet limited to travel by foot or by horse**, Asia Minor would be at the outer limits of his travel and his imagination. Russia did not exist. And if the word "uttermost" was merely a relative term in their time of limited geographic knowledge, the list of northern invaders of Israel was long: Assyrians, Babylonians, Persians, Greeks (Alexander the Great), Romans, and more.

Gog and Magog

Could God expand the primitive prophet's imagination? Yes, but the track record shows that God rarely gave any such anachronistic preview to the Bible writers. God revealed God's Word with a great restraint, with a respect for the cultural limits of the human hands who would write down the divinely-inspired words. With the exception of a few spots in Scripture (such as the Ten Commandments written in stone and handed to Moses, and the words of Jesus), God did not dictate exact words or reduce the Bible writers to mere stenographers or secretaries. God embodied his revelation through a more subtle inspiration, merging it with the life experiences of the writers/prophets and their place in history. So in their view, the world was limited mostly to the Mediterranean, and there is not a hint of modern history being spelled out in the visions God gave them: nothing like an airplane, car, electricity or the like. For example, the Prophet Daniel describes the future war waged by the antichrist as using "siege ramps" and "chariots."
In Ezekiel's description about the horrible future war that is coming (in the 20th Century, according to Lindsey), the prophet specifically refers to the weapons in use as "the bows and the arrows" and other wooden weapons of Ezekiel's time period. All the weapons, after the battle, will be piled up and burned, he foresaw, with a fire that will last for seven years.

AK47's don't burn... and while gunpowder and gas will burn, the fire won't last seven days, much less seven years. Yet Lindsey would have us believe that in this one matter, Ezekiel was inspired by God to describe a country that would not exist for centuries... even while in every other aspect of the prediction, the prophet's vision is limited to describing his own time and culture. Most of Ezekiel's references regarding persons and places are identifiable as ones of his immediate surroundings, his own *Sitz im Leben*, his own time and place—not someone/someplace in the distant and mysterious future.

Linguistic Guessing Games

The truth is, there are just **not** enough specifics given in the ancient Scripture to positively identify Gog and Magog. Most of Lindsey's attempts to identify Gog and Magog as the main players in a Final War against Israel are based on word similarities of *Rosh* to *Russia* and *Meshech* to *Moscow*... a stretch at best, and not rooted in archaeological or historical studies. Citing the passage (Ezekiel 38) most used by the Gog=Russia crowd, the well-respected and moderate *Interpreter's Dictionary* unequivocally states that Gog and Magog have "no relationship to Russia, nor does Meshech refer to Moscow."[28] That was written long before Lindsey would write, to the contrary, that Ezekiel's "Meshech" is the namesake of Moscow. The image of Russia descending upon Israel was quite a convincing scenario in the Seventies, but after the dissolution of the USSR, and the U.S. conquering Iraq (the path to Israel that an invading USSR would have taken), Lindsey's case became less compelling. Now, with the rise of Islam as the seemingly-greater threat, one of his fellow propheteers, Joel Richardson, argues against Gog/Magog being identified with Russia. He cites respected Bible scholar Dr. Merrill F. Unger, who wrotes, "Linguistic evidence for the equation [of Gog with Rosh, and Rosh with

Russia] is confessedly only presumptive."[29] In other words, a guess unsupported by scholarship.

However, even when Lindsey published his best-seller in 1970, I would have then still asked him, "If Ezekiel 38 applies to modern Israel (as the victim of Gog's attack), how do you explain 38:11, where this prophecy refers to Israel as a 'land of unwalled villages...having no bars or gates'?" That does *not* describe modern Israel by any stretch of the imagination. Modern Israel is a land *filled* with walls, checkpoints, fences, gates and other barriers. Compare the Israel described by Ezekiel with this headline from NBCNews.com on March 20th, 2013: "Israel becomes a fortress nation as it walls itself off...." Lindsey loves to juxtapose modern headlines with Scripture—when it fits his scenario. You can bet he never mentioned the description of an unwalled, un-gated Israel in Ezekiel 38:11 alongside that headline above, or with photos of the 500 miles of fences and gates in modern Israel. Incidentally, in a much newer book, Joel Richardson makes the same mistake. Also speaking of Ezekiel 38, he writes: "Clearly Ezekiel was describing the Israel of today."[30] I have no doubt the prophet was referring to Israel... but his description certainly does NOT match the walled "Israel of today."

Selective verse-picking and misapplication seem to go hand in hand with the End Timers' eagerness to sell their story. But it is about more than just money. Behind all this hide psychological drives: the desire for hope that "our team will win in the end," the curiosity about our future, and the "big themes" of life, such as morality, war, religion and death... the word Carl Jung uses for the latter is *archetype*.

C. G. Jung and Apocalyptic Vision
Dr. Carl G. Jung was a brilliant visionary with an encyclopedic knowledge of literature, philosophy, religion and psychology. He was certainly not an orthodox Christian,

but the Swiss psychologist, a son of a Protestant minister, studied the Bible as much as the average TV evangelist. Unlike his secularist rival, Sigmund Freud, Dr. Jung believed in God and in the existence of a spiritual realm. He called it the "collective unconscious," and he taught that one way we make contact with that spiritual realm is via *Archetypes*. Jung identified these as universal prototypes of ideas, "primordial images" representing key concepts about human life and revelatory of God's purposes. Archetypes manifest as constantly recurring symbols or motifs in literature, art, mythology, and even in our dreams. Those motifs reflect deep truths of human existence.

Jung also wrote a great deal on the topic of Apocalyptic visions, understanding them as a recurring, foundational, archetypal idea found in a variety of cultures and religions across the centuries. End of Time visions, according to Jung, are full of archetypal motifs: angelic beings in a circular craft descending from heaven (in Ezekiel); giantism; trees; rocks and mountains (in Daniel); serpent/dragon; blood and death; the Trickster/Satan (in Revelation); expansive seas; astronomical events in the sun, moon and stars; fire, darkness and light (in all three). These images of eschatology run deep and wide in the social collective unconsciousness.

Do not dismiss this chapter as "Psych 101 mumbo-jumbo." When I bring psychology into this discussion, let me be clear. I am NOT being dismissive. I am NOT saying that End Time visions, prophecies and ideas are merely a projection or a product of a psychological need. Whether or not people yearn for a particular religious concept **has no bearing on whether that concept is true or false!** Jesus will either come again in physical form, or as some Christians believe, He will not come physically but has already "returned" allegorically, into the human heart. The method of Christ's return is not based on what we feel or want. No, my point here is to explain **a)** the richness of apocalyptic vision, as something that speaks to our deepest spiritual and psychological selves, and **b)** to help explain the motives of End Times readers. Why do audiences continue to buy books and movies on this subject even when the propheteers have been proven wrong time and time again? Of all religious topics, perhaps even more than "love and marriage," End Times books outsell them all. One reason for this is found in Dr. Jung's work.

Our Lost Transcendence

Jung speaks of the "numinous," a term related to a similar word, transcendence. The numinous is the spiritual side of existence, it is that which cannot be seen by the outer eye, but felt and engaged with the inner depths, usually with emotional intensity. I agree with Dr. Jung on this: true spiritual experience must be more than mere emotions. **Emotionalism should never be mistaken for true spiritualism.** But when we engage the numinous, it requires a transcendent experience, and this in turn often engages, in a very powerful way, our emotions and our sub-conscious selves. One reason religion has been such a huge and influential part of human history is that we have an intense longing for that transcendent experience—and religion helps us engage it. Put another way: we long to experience something deeper than surface reality.

But now our modern psyches are alienated from the numinous. In this post-enlightenment, post-modernity era, we have lost a daily sense of the divine. Transcendent vision has been largely supplanted by electronic vision. We live in an age inundated by visual media (TV/video, computer screens, video games, etc.). Saint Paul encountered a blinding, life-changing light on the road to Damascus; our light emitting diodes (LEDs) are a tiny, pale substitute. Thus, society is starving for a grand numinous vision... and there is nothing grander than the CinemaScopic vision of St. John's *Apocalypse* (Revelation). The biblical visions of End Times are full of color and symbol, the vistas are vast, the characters bigger than life, the themes are at once primordial and futuristic. There is something deeply satisfying when one makes an attachment to such a vision of such a grand scale. A sheep farmer in a small church in Montana reads a passage from Revelation, and suddenly he feels connected to something larger and more significant than his mundane spot in life.

Why the End of the World is so Attractive

Throughout my 30 years of ministry, I taught a weekly Bible Study (apart from the Sunday sermon). I usually would spend a month or two focused solely on a single book of the Bible, and over time, I tried to cover a wide variety of both Old and New Testament books. At the various parishes I served, whether urban or rural, when I taught a study on Revelation, the attendance would double. The interest was keen for the first several sessions, but soon the parishioners came to understand this was a relatively-dry and somewhat-academic study of the book, lacking dragon props and no fancy 7-year Tribulation charts, and so attendance flagged. I simply wasn't able to present the transcendent vision to them. Ironically, *movies* about the End Times do a better job of that! (Better emotionally, I mean, not better in terms of accuracy.) It is difficult to transmit to another person a religious vision—especially the most moving and powerful vision imaginable—without a movie screen.

This brings us back to the problem faced by the Bible writers. They experienced their visions in an impassioned, multi-dimensional way: not only visually/audibly full of colors, full of sound and fury, but also full *emotionally*. So when they tried to pass their visceral visions onto us with mere words on a page, power was lost in translation. What must be even more frustrating for those Bible prophets is to now see Christians oblivious to the sound and fury, instead focusing on the script as if it were a mere weather report, looking for a forecast of dates, times and temperatures. With the exception of the Pentateuch, the Bible writers were not stenographers, they were visionaries and their words are not from a Dictabelt, but from heart and spirit.

Revelatory, Not Riddling

Think about this: the way the modern propheteers approach these eschatological Bible passages is as if they were riddles. But the Bible is not a parlor game. This is not a game of "guess my age and weight." The reason God uses the archetypal images, the grand visual symbolism found in Daniel, Ezekiel and Revelation, is **not to *obscure* the future, but to reveal it**, and the revelation given in those visions is not about guessing dates and times. The numbers are really not intended (in most of the prophetic passages) as *counting* numbers, but as *symbolic* numbers. The critic might claim that Revelation 13:18, regarding the antichrist "code" of 666, is indeed a riddle, because that verse encourages us to "calculate the number of the beast." But even in that one case, the riddle is the opposite of the propheteers' numbers game: the number is a code that leads us to a person, not to another date or number. 6 is the number of sinful man. The number 3 points to God the Trinity; the number 7 is perfection and holiness; the number 40, used throughout the Bible, is symbolic of a period in which God is working purposefully... it is not intended to be taken as a literal mathematical number. This is why all the propheteers' methods of date prediction have failed: **in sum, the revelatory visions are not about historical dating, they are about something bigger, they are about a spiritual message**. And the message is about the big themes... not about *when* but about *WHOM*... who God is. The visions of Daniel and John tell us that God is supreme, God is love, God has a plan for the future, God is Good, and Good will triumph over death and war. That is the more important message of divine revelation, and to seek otherwise is to contradict three clear commands from Jesus:

1. Do not worry about tomorrow. (Matthew 6:34)
2. Do not seek a sign. (Matthew 12:38-39)
3. Spend energy on personal spiritual preparation, not on trying to know what date God will choose to bring this world's era to an end. Only God knows. (Mark 13:32)

~~~

Chapter Ten: *Left Behind, or Right Ahead?* Political Bias and the End Times Movement

"There is a way that seems right to a man, But its end is the way of death."
  ~*Proverbs 14:12*

"Now this was the sin of your sister Sodom: She and her daughters were arrogant, overfed and unconcerned; they did not help the poor and needy."
  ~*Ezekiel 16:49*

"They are shepherds who lack understanding; they all turn to their own way, they seek their own gain."
  ~*Isaiah 56:11*

  LaHaye, Lindsey, Hagee and their comrades not only pontificate about *religion*, they also want to share their views on *politics*. Loudly. For a variety of reasons—some social/psychological and some mysterious— 90% of them are ultra-conservative... overtly members of the political Right. If you consider yourself conservative, I ask you to be open-minded and not view this as an attack on your ideology. As a Southern, Bible-believing Christian, I'm a mix of conservative, moderate and liberal—depending on the issue. All I ask for is a balanced approach as we raise concerns about the all-or-nothing extremism, intolerance and exclusiveness found in too many of the End Times books.
  The point of this chapter is three-fold:
1. When End-Timers show their extreme political bias, this raises doubts about their credibility;
2. Their arrogance and tunnel-vision is not grounded in reality, and is in conflict with the Christ-like ethics of grace and humility;
3. Fretting over the "secularization" of our government and the perceived "war on Christianity" is not warranted by the facts, and interferes with our ability to reach Left-leaning

progressives for Christ. God wants Liberals in His Church, too! So I plead with readers to be open-minded about this chapter, and in humility, be willing to consider that you may have been taught just one side of the End Times perspective.

Humility is Hard

One would imagine that, with a thousand year history of repeated failure, End Time authors might have found a bit of humility. Alas, no. Instead, they **not only emphatically assert their "rightness," they also denigrate anyone with a different opinion.** The narrow vision and self-righteousness of Stone, Hagee, LaHaye, *et al*, is especially evident when it comes to their eschatological overlap into politics. They almost always support the far-right Republican Party, or, with some irony, conservative Libertarians. That alone would be fine... but they go further. They cannot tolerate those of us with a varying political view, they allow no room in Christendom for political moderates. They make it very clear that Republicans are Godly Christians while Democrats are agents of Satan. I'm not exaggerating here for effect; their writings are emphatic on the matter, and their religious intolerance is not far from being a mirror image of the Taliban (in labeling opponents as "Satanic").

A quick example of this religious-political arrogance: it is not enough for Perry Stone to insist, as he does, that America is a "Christian nation." He *deprecates* any other view, **insulting anyone who differs from his assertions**. Anyone with a different understanding, anyone who sees history from a different angle than Stone, he labels either as evil or ignorant. He wrote that anyone who denies that the U.S. started out as a Christian theocracy is guilty of "an attempt to cover up, willful lying, or complete historical ignorance."

I happen to disagree with him, quite strongly in fact... and I am not ignorant, I am not a liar, I am not trying to cover anything up. I'm an honest Christian who has carefully read the historical record. **Our forebears had varied opinions on the subject.** At least half the signers of our founding documents were **not** orthodox Christians (by what Stone himself would define as such). Many were self-confessed agnostics and atheists, a few were Jewish, but a significant percentage were just Deists who did not subscribe to any specific Christian creed. And even of those who were self-professed orthodox Christians, few wanted the new country to be identified as a solely Christian nation. I would dare say that in total, 80% of the Founders would have strongly opposed making America a "Christian theocracy." I am aware that there are plenty of quotes to be found in the archives where some individuals called our then-budding country a "Christian nation." The owners of the *Hobby Lobby* chain-store run a full-page ad in major newspapers every 4th of July, citing those quotes in order to claim that "America is a Christian nation." Their ad fails to mention that many *more* quotes from founders are also dotted throughout the historical record, quotes that plainly state the contrary: we are a nation whose government favors no particular religion. We treasure religious freedom.

What the Founders Really Said
•**President George Washington**, 1789: "...no one would be more zealous than myself to establish effectual barriers against the horrors of spiritual tyranny, and every species of religious persecution."
•Baptist clergyman and pilgrim colonist **Roger Williams** was the first in the New World to use the phrase, a "wall of separation" between church and state, and he explained the need for it: "An enforced uniformity of religion throughout a nation or civil state, confounds the civil and religious, and denies the principles of Christianity...." He should know. Rev. Williams had his own religious convictions that, while Christian, were not exactly congruent with the Puritans who

ran the Massachusetts Bay Colony. Those who disagreed with the "state religion" could be whipped or imprisoned. Williams was threatened with exile, so in 1636 he moved to what would become Rhode Island, where he established the first Baptist Church in America and chartered the first colony that guaranteed complete religious freedom for everyone.
•**President Thomas Jefferson**, in 1802, echoed Rev. Williams' phrase and used it to explain the purpose of the First Amendment: "building a wall of separation between church and state." And in 1813: "I am for freedom of religion and against… a legal ascendancy of one sect over another.... History, I believe, furnishes no example of a priest-ridden people maintaining a free civil government. This marks the lowest grade of ignorance...."
•**President James Madison**, 1819: "The civil government functions with complete success by the total separation of the Church from the State." "Torrents of blood have been spilt in the old world, by vain attempts of the [governments there] to extinguish Religious discord, by proscribing all difference in Religious opinion." (Again, a chief reason people fled Europe for American shores was because they were sick of kings and governments dictating the form of their religion.)
•**Founding Father Alexander Hamilton**, 1791: "What is far more precious than mere religious toleration? A perfect equality of religious privileges...."
•**John Leland**, Baptist minister of the 1700's and influential with the Founders: "The notion of a Christian commonwealth should be exploded forever...all should be equally free: Jews, Turks, Pagans and Christians. If government can answer for individuals at the day of judgment, let men be controlled by it in religious matters; otherwise, let men be free."
•**Founding Father George Mason**, 1776: "...religion... can be directed only by reason and conviction, not by force or violence; and therefore all men are equally entitled to the free exercise of religion...."

- **Patriot Patrick Henry**, 1766: "A general toleration of Religion appears to me the best means of peopling our country… The free exercise of religion hath stocked the Northern part of the continent with inhabitants...."
- **Founding Father Oliver Wolcott**, 1788: "Knowledge and liberty are so prevalent in this country, that I do not believe that the United States would ever be disposed to establish one religious sect...." Nevertheless, he argued in favor of the First and Fifth Amendments to make sure the Constitution "...secures us from the possibility of such oppression."
- **Founding Father Noah Webster**: Government "...ought to have given every honest citizen an equal right to enjoy his religion and an equal title to all civil emoluments, without obliging him to tell his religion. Every interference of the civil power in regulating opinion is an impious attempt to take the business of the Deity out of his own hands...."

I realize that the fans of theocracy can counter with their own "founding fathers" quotes, such as this one from **John Adams**: "The general principles on which the fathers achieved independence were the general principles of Christianity." But that is not the same as asserting we are a "Christian nation" or demanding government teach religion in schools. While President, John Adams made no attempt to enshrine Christianity as a state religion, and in fact, he signed the 1797 Treaty of Tripoli that states: "The Government of the United States of America is not in any sense founded on the Christian religion."

Our laws, founding documents and governmental structure derive almost as much from Judaism, Freemasonry and Enlightenment-era Secularist philosophy as they do from Christian tradition. If anything, our founding patriots and our founding documents were collectively a **mongrel religion**, and certainly not the peculiar purebred of contemporary evangelical "pop" Christianity we see today.

Who Decides?

So who should decide this matter? The ultimate arbiter of our Laws is the **Supreme Court**, and it has clearly and repeatedly proclaimed two facts in the matter:

1. That vague and generic references to "God" and "Providence" as well as ceremonial, non-sectarian public prayers are permissible.
2. And that in no way can a government entity be involved in the business of church nor in the act of endorsing or promulgating any specific faith/religion.

Moreover, the ultimate Law of our Land, the **U.S. Constitution**, is a secular document, and like the Declaration of Independence, it never mentions Christianity. The Constitution refers to religion only twice, both times for the explicit purpose of prohibiting a theocracy! In its First Amendment, it forbids any governmental action "respecting [favoring one over another] an establishment of religion," and in Article VI, it forbids "religious tests" for candidates for public office.

Yet Perry Stone wants to assert that I am "ignorant" or a liar for denying that we are a Christian nation? We are a nation *influenced* by Christianity and *containing* a lot of Christian people, but that is not the same as "a Christian nation." Somalia and Iran are **Muslim nations**: their theocratic governments openly persecute Christians and coerce citizens to follow Muhammad. By contrast, the United States of America purposely welcome citizens of all faiths, or of no faith, and we have institutionally guaranteed that all religions here get equal treatment by the ruling powers. Personally, I am proud of that contrast. If the U.S. were a "Christian nation," i.e. a Christian theocracy, that would not be the opposite of a Muslim nation... we would be a mirror image, erring in exactly the same manner, albeit with a different name.

Lazy Christians?

The God I serve is not threatened by diverse beliefs, nor is so weak that He needs the power of the State to impose the message of faith (if that were even possible). Asking for a Christian government or theocracy to pave our spiritual path is a lazy way out. Anyone who believes strongly (as do I) that Christianity is "the way, the truth and the life," should use their free speech rights to proclaim it in the appropriate venues, and should encourage children to attend church and religious education. It is lazy and imprudent to ask the government to impose some brief, meaningless, watered-down prayer upon schoolchildren via some public school teacher who may have not an ounce of real knowledge of real religion. I attended public schools before the day when, as conservatives claim, "they took Jesus out of the schools." The only teacher I remember strongly telling us about God was also the same teacher who tried to convince us that the Ku Klux Klan was a good thing. Conversely, my daughters "survived" modern "godless" public schools. They of course were not forbidden to pray at school (they did so silently), and in fact attended Christian club meetings on campus, as allowed by law... and grew up to be fine, committed Christians.

The pilgrims, the founders of what would become the United States, sailed here to escape Old World countries where the king or government tried to impose a particular brand of faith upon them. They were seeking religious freedom, not a government-defined orthodoxy.

I'm not digressing from our topic here; I'm proving my point that Stone's assertion is, at the very least, highly debatable. Therefore it is arrogant for him to insist that his opinion is a dogmatic fact. I am also asking conservative readers to view this as a "thought exercise." Ask yourself honestly: "Has my emotional desire to live in an all-Christian nation colored my thinking?" I find Christian conservatives often have never thoroughly examined both sides of the issue of Church and State. They feel strongly that our government should be Christian, but they would howl loudly if the shoe were on the other foot and they found themselves a minority in a Muslim or Hindu country. Jesus commanded, "Do unto others as you would have them do unto you." Does that not require us to treat other religions as we would want ourselves to be treated, if Christians were in the minority?

If you were surprised by the quotes from our founding fathers (above), which I find to be convincing proof that America was *not* designed to be exclusively "a Christian nation," what does that say about your biases? If you have spent most of your life within evangelical circles, reading only books with a Rightwing view, is it not also possible that your previous thinking on End Times theory was also biased?

The political bias of the End Timers can be seen in many more ways. I'll cite just a few more.

"Christian?" Militarism

The glorification of war found among apocalyptic authors reveals an unsettling bias, a dark place in politics. Their extreme Rightwing militaristic view is quite evident in their lust for blood-soaked Armageddon scenes. Do you think I exaggerate? Consider this: Tim LaHaye licensed the rights to the violent video game, "Left Behind: Eternal Forces." The computer game is a "Christian" real-time strategy game based on his *Left Behind* series of novels, in which players are encouraged to act out mass murder on non-Christians. Attorney Jack Thompson, himself a Christian, strongly criticized the violence in the video game, pointing out that "The game is about killing people for their lack of faith in Jesus." His complaint is significant considering he shared the same publisher with LaHaye; he subsequently severed his ties with *Left Behind* publisher Tyndale House, citing the video game as antithetical to true Christianity.

Whether it be games, movies or books, the apocalyptic entertainment business comes all too close to a self-fulfilling prophecy, affecting real life. Hal Lindsey lectured Pentagon officials, encouraging them to view the Middle East through the lens of an imminent Armageddon. He wrote the same sentence in two of his books, *Planet Earth 2000 A.D.* (1994) and *The Final Battle* (1995): "The greatest threat to freedom and world peace today is Islamic fundamentalism.... Tragically, the world's sole remaining superpower—the United States—has responded to this monumental threat by embarking on a suicidal, unilateral demilitarization process of unprecedented speed and recklessness." This Republican-perpetrated myth, that "liberal" Presidents have made us weak, is dangerous nonsense. From WWII up until today, the U.S. has not wavered from being the biggest and most technologically advanced military force on earth. The U.S. spends almost as much as **the entire rest of the world combined** on defense. We spend over four times as much annually on defense as China. Our Air Force and Navy dwarf our enemies.' We have the *only* truly worldwide Navy, and our Air Force was almost untouched as it bombed Hussein's Iraq back to the Stone Age. There is no comparison. Let's consider tanks. The M1 Abrams tank has seen more combat than just about any other modern tank. Not a single one has ever been destroyed by enemy fire. Ever. China has less than 500 of its T-99 tanks. We have 8,700 Abrams.

During the first campaign of Ronald Reagan, Republican campaigners tried to paint Democrats as weak on defense, telling the lie that the USSR had a stronger military than ours. It was not true then, and it is not true today.[31] We have 20 aircraft carriers. Russia has one. We have over four times the number of aircraft as they do. And nuclear? We had 32,000 nuclear warheads/bombs at the peak of the Cold War. One warhead could effectively destroy a city. A "mere" 2,000 would destroy every major city and military base in

Russia *and* China. Why did we build an additional 30,000 at a cost of trillions?[32] Nevertheless, the propheteers keep churning up fear, keep making taxpayers fearful so we don't revolt against the bloated, greedy military-industrial complex... which is absurd, since even if the End Times scenario *were* to unfold as the propheteers warn, our weapons would be useless in the supernatural war between Jesus and the antichrist! Where is your faith? In angels or in warheads?

Christian Zionists

Lindsey, LaHaye, Stone, Cahn and Hagee have another important matching view in the political realm: they are strongly pro-Zionist. Let me be clear: I'm all for helping Israel survive. We should indeed help our allies, and Israel is a strong ally surrounded by hostile countries. The Jewish people have a history of enduring extreme persecution that warrants our sympathetic support. With that said, we still cannot turn a blind eye to atrocities committed by the Israeli government, we cannot hand them Carte Blanche. We give a huge amount of money and military aid to Israel, even before we count the dollars spent on additional military efforts in the Middle East, much of which benefits Israel. Thus we should have some input into how Israel wields that power.

Jonathan Cahn, who is the Christian leader of the "Jerusalem Center/Beth Israel," wrote: "There is no nation in the modern world so deeply linked to ancient Israel as America." He and others believe that America is a New Jerusalem, a new chosen nation. He fails to note that the "Christian Identity" movement, with its ironic name but its desire to identify America with Israel, first asserted that the British Isles were the new Israel. So Cahn overstates. But he continues: "If America ever turned away from God, then the same judgments that fell upon ancient Israel would fall upon America." This is, of course, pure speculation, since Scripture never mentions the U.S., and since the curses and warnings of the Old Testament are no longer in effect. "God forgave us all our sins, having canceled the charge of our legal indebtedness [the Jewish legal requirements]… nailing it to the cross." (Colossians 2:13-14)

Neither Cahn nor his cohorts seem to think that *modern* Israel has any flaws. Cahn, Lindsey and Hagee apparently believe that Israel, being God's chosen people, can do no wrong. The irony here is that if we read the Bible, we find God frequently and vehemently chiding Israel for disobedience, disloyalty and gross sin. Lindsey and Hagee treat the Israeli government as if it were a band of angels. How much material benefit (whether it be money, subsidized trips to the Holy Land, or promotion of their books) have Lindsey and Hagee gained by way of their chummy relationship with Israel? Is Israel an underprivileged country in need of this evangelical boosterism? Hagee thinks so. He's the founder and National Chairman of *Christians United for Israel*, a Zionist advocacy organization that raises money to promote the idea that we have a biblical obligation to militarily defend Israel.

Often their political extremes create ironical contradictions. Right-leaning evangelicals, generally speaking, think Jews are going to Hell if they don't accept Jesus Christ... yet most of the End Time propheteers are Pro-Zionist. They also claim to be flag-waving U.S. patriots of the type who scream, "America first!" Yet one wonders where their allegiance lies: with God, with the U.S., or with Israel? The three are not always in agreement.

Fear God or Fear the Antichrist?

Another irony among Rightwing Christians: they pronounce with great authority and emphasis that **God is all-powerful**, yet they seem to live in **fear** that government is more powerful than God. Cahn, for example, wrote: "Israel had begun driving God out of its government, out of its public squares, out of its culture.... America has done likewise—beginning in the early 1960s as America banned prayer and the reading of Scripture from its public schools."[33] That reveals a theology of a very weak God, who can be "driven out" by a simple government decree to show no favoritism in the field of religion. Can any government stop prayer in school? Of course not. As one joke goes, whenever a teacher announces to her 30 students an unexpected and difficult quiz, 30 prayers are instantly lifted up in school: "*Please* help me pass this test, O Lord!"

Fear of Government, Little Support for Social Programs

So what is the problem with the End-Time philosophy being inserted into politics? First, it creates an unhelpful, unhealthy pessimism (also discussed in other chapters herein). Second, it fosters an anti-government, anti-progressive suspicion that hampers social progress. I'm willing to concede, this isn't all bad! A healthy skepticism about government being our "savior" may serve us well. (One of the Three Big Lies is: "I'm from the government, and I'm here to help you.") Nevertheless, when one has a pessimistic view—that the government is evil and is setting the stage for an antichrist— this rules out any hope for social progress. Many fine and good programs get dismissed *a priori*, instead of being measured rationally by their value. I'm not overstating. In the Thirties, a large minority opposed the imposition of a Social Security Number because they feared it would be the "mark or number of the Beast." Social Security is universally viewed now as a wonderful social good, and I can't imagine how it could operate without each citizen having a unique number. (I will admit, however, that I would refuse to allow them to tattoo it on my forehead!)

The "Left Behind" movie series does not bother to create a fictional evil; it outright names the United Nations as the evil partner-army for the antichrist! Again, it is fine to hold the

UN accountable to be an honest organization, but to demonize it by associating it with a (future) dictator who is seen as even more evil than Hitler, is unethical. UN peacekeepers, from a wide variety of freedom-loving nations, have died in order to help keep the peace. If the UN ever seems to be becoming more powerful than our own nation, we can have a different conversation, but for now, to utterly demonize one of the more positive, peacekeeping organizations on the planet is irresponsible.

Politics and Religion Make Strange Bedfellows

Another political irony: Hagee was eager to support Mitt Romney for President, even though Mitt is a devout member of a group that Hagee had previously *condemned* as an un-Christian cult. This contradiction is not so surprising when we consider that Romney is white and Obama, Romney's rival, is black. Is Hagee a bigot? Based on things he has said in the past, we could make that argument. But one thing we do know for certain: he is a false prophet who has used Christianity and "prophecy" to enrich himself at levels more like a celebrity or CEO than a pastor.

In his book, *Deciphering End-Time Prophetic Codes*, Perry Stone includes a long digression from the topic to lament how America is becoming "socialist," citing the Affordable Care Act as an example of "evil" socialism. While there are indeed some aspects of our government that might be deemed socialist, that is not one of them. Any informed and fair critic would have to admit that Obamacare was a compromise engineered by capitalist forces including private insurance companies, Big Pharma, and healthcare providers, and is not remotely like true socialistic medical programs found in Britain and Canada. His attacks reek of partisanship: George Bush's expansion of the Medicare drug program could just as easily be called "socialized medicine," but to my knowledge, Stone never opposed it.

When you make the kind of excessively-high income that Hagee and LaHaye reap, you would naturally want to support Republicans who protect them from progressive taxation. I say "naturally" only from the Christian perspective of our natural fallen state of greed and selfishness. If they were truly Christ-like they would be happy to share their wealth. Their diversion into these political arenas, which have very little to do with the topic of End Times, reveals their true colors.

Hyper Hyperbole: Obama = Hitler?

Perry Stone's slanted ranting even goes so far as to overtly call President Obama an Adolf Hitler twin... Stone makes no attempt to hide his extremely partisan, Rightwing view. Consider Stone's take on income inequality. Rather than mentioning that taxation on the wealthy is now way lower than historic highs, or the fact that middle class wages have stagnated over the last 30 years (while the rich got vastly richer), he instead bemoans that the richest "One percent of Americans pay $1Trillion in tax revenue." Simply not true. Stone is contradicted even by those who share his political bias! According to the conservative "Tax Foundation," the top **50** percent (not even close to Stone's 1%) of taxpayers paid $1.01 trillion in income taxes.[34] And his absurd figure of $1Trillion makes no sense as a *percentage*, either: based on his own figure of $2.5 trillion for total Federal revenue, he is claiming the top 1% pay 40% of all tax revenue. But the fact is that the richest 1% pay only 24% (according to tax receipt data from the Congressional Budget Office for 2011).[35] This is part of his imagined script of how, under Obama, we are spiraling into communism. Problem is, his script on politics is just as fictional as his script on the End Times. Not only does Stone give fictional numbers on the amount of taxes paid by the rich, he also fails to tell the rest of the story: that in that same year, the richest of the rich—the 1%—kept *twice* the money, after taxes, as they did in 1978! So the rich are getting vastly richer, which is an opposite scenario from the yarn Stone spins.

   He rants for two chapters about our terrible slide, like Nazi Germany and ancient Rome, into socialist societies that (supposedly) milked the rich. But if Stone's script were accurate, why does all the data prove conclusively that the rich are getting MUCH richer while the poor and middle class have been in wage stagnation for these past 30 years?! In other words, Stone is not merely politically biased—he is deceiving the reader. It is not a typo or careless exaggeration. He also claims that "only 40 percent of the population pays any type of taxes." This is another lie, because he surely knows that even retirees and those in poverty who don't pay Federal income tax still have to pay all sorts of other taxes: ALL workers pay social security tax, medicare tax, sales tax, special taxes on utilities and cellphone, a huge gasoline tax, and a variety of other excise taxes. These taxes, unlike income taxes, are not progressive… the poor pay as much tax on groceries as the millionaires do.

Income Inequality
   Which points up the bigger flaw in the End-Timers' argument: Stone (and Hagee, who has similar "complaints" about high taxation on high earners) ignores the inarguable fact that the working class pays a far higher *percentage* of their income in taxes… their burden is heavy while the load carried by the rich is light. According to The Corporation for Enterprise Development, if we look at all taxes beyond Federal income tax, in states with the most regressive taxes, the poorest 20% pay over five times the rate of the richest 1%.[36] In my own state of Alabama, for example, low-income families who make less than $13,000 pay 11% of their income in state and local taxes, while those making more than $229,000 pay just 4 percent, thanks to deductions and loopholes. So as Hagee, LaHaye and Stone moan about their

horrible tax burden, the truth is that the working poor have to worry everyday about whether they can pay their bills—a fear that the wealthy authors never have to face.

What accounts for the fact that these End Times writers often side with the 1% and the 1%'s favorite political party (Republicans)? Could it be they feel more affinity with the ultra-wealthy, as opposed to the poor "least of these" that Jesus loves so much?

~~~

Chapter Eleven: *Hope vs. Despair*
Is There a Future for the Church?

"There is surely a future hope for you, and your hope will not be cut off."
   ~*Proverbs 23:18*

Jesus said: "...on this rock I will build my Church, and the gates of Hell will not overcome it."
   ~*Matthew 16:18b*

When I read the cocksure arrogant proclamations in many of the End Times books, when I observed the gloating and glee about being one of the Chosen Few who are to be raptured whilst the "pagans" are left behind to burn in agony, I find that a striking contrast to the command of Colossians 3:12: "As God's chosen people... clothe yourselves with compassion, kindness, humility, gentleness and patience." The great British theologian, C.S. Lewis, warned: "Whenever we find that our religious life is making us feel that we are good— above all, that we are *better* than someone else—I think we may be sure that we are being acted on not by God, but by the devil."

Sodomites and Pessimists

Perhaps I should apologize for writing about "End-Timers" in monolithic terms, as if they were of a single mind. Of course there are exceptions, but frankly, my generalizations *do* fit the vast majority of the propheteers. Another common thread amongst almost all of them is this: they invariably cite an increasing moral corruption of society as a sure sign of impending doom. And their diagnosis of our moral decay is consistent with their ultra-conservative ideology; their list of sins usually begins with homosexuality, abortion and other sex-related vices. Violence, greed and income inequality do not seem to be high on their "sin concern list." On this one point, I give credit to Perry Stone, as he does cite "greed" in his list of growing societal sins. But even with Stone, in the end, it is our sin-similarity to "Sodom and Gomorrah" that concerns him the most. (I do agree that raping angels, as the Sodomites attempted to do, could tick God off.) It is interesting to note, however, that while the self-righteous Rightwingers focus solely on the *sexual* sins in Sodom, Ezekiel had a different focus. Ezekiel 16:49 used the terms "lewdness and abominations" and "unfaithfulness," but applied these to Samaria and Jerusalem, **not to Sodom**. Ezekiel added: "Now this was the sin of your sister Sodom: She and her daughters were arrogant, overfed and unconcerned; they did not help the poor and needy." Here Ezekiel sounds more like a Liberal! When Rightwingers make their lists of societal sins that are bringing Judgment upon us, you will not find economic inequality on the list— even though it is a primary concern of most Old Testament prophets and of Jesus in the Gospels (especially His words in the Gospel of Luke). [For a more in-depth look at what the Bible has to say about income inequality, I highly recommend the book, *Class Crucifixion: Money, Power, Religion and the Death of the Middle Class*, an incisive tome on social ethics by a brilliant author. Wink.]

Are We Really on the Highway to Hell?

Is modern society truly in decay at a faster rate than previous generations? I doubt it. We don't have accurate records from antiquity, but **crime rates** (rape, murder, burglary and more) **have all *decreased*** over the last 30 years.[37] What we do see in our time is a much easier access to the *knowledge* of crimes, more media coverage of atrocities, and at the same time, a greater public acceptance of "victimless crimes" that once were considered "horrible sins"... for example, in the fifties, homosexuals were routinely imprisoned for sodomy in Britain. In the Fifties and

Sixties, racy movies left more to the imagination, so the outer veneer of society might have appeared more Victorian. Now the Internet and cable/satellite TV have made pornography available with a few clicks of the mouse or the remote, so we are certainly more aware of it. But do the End Timers honestly think that no one wanted to look at nudity 100 years ago, or that teenagers didn't have sex 200 years ago, or that there were not similar percentages of practicing homosexuals 1,000 years ago?

It may bother us that nowadays young people say the word "f#ck" with the casualness that my generation spoke the word "darn," and it may bother us that the nudes our parents once hid under the mattress in the pages of Playboy are now shown nightly on HBO... but perhaps our increasing "lack of shame" is counterbalanced by a decrease in our hypocrisy and repressed secrecy. Did humanity hit the depths of human evil and depravity with the toilet humor of today's *Southpark* cartoons, or in the 1940's with Hitler's gas chambers, genocidal holocaust and razed earth warfare, or with the atomic bomb's utter annihilation of civilian women and children? It's been over sixty years since then and thankfully nothing has come close to the scale of evil spewed in World War II. So on what basis are the End Timers saying that now, today, we are suddenly more depraved than the last 4,000 years of human greed, lust and bloody violence?

A Dim View of the Golden Age?

I am not arguing that humanity is progressing toward a golden age. Atrocities continue. I do, however, think that myths of a prior golden age (outside of Eden) are wishful pipedreams... or sentimental hogwash. When people long for "the good old days," what era are they referring to? The Civil War, when humans were enslaved and the carnage at Gettysburg left 50,000 casualties and "7,000 slain men and 3,000 dead horses—an estimated 6 million lbs. of human and animal carcasses—lay strewn," rotting, stinking and full of maggots, "across the field in the summer heat."?[38] Or do the End-Timers long for the Prohibition era, when the government mandated sanctimonious sobriety, but millions ignored the order and Al Capone and his ilk supplied the speak-easy saloons via blood-splattered gang wars? If we return to those pre-modernity "golden years" of imagined moral purity, does that also mean that women and blacks must surrender their right to vote, or that we should return to Charles Dickens' days of dark and cruel child labor? It truly takes a pessimist to think that America is in such dire spiritual decline today that God is firing up His Armageddon machine to mow us down... after turning a blind eye to Napoleon, Stalin, and Hitler for all those years.

Do we need more love and less hate today? Yes, please! But crying doomsday wolf is not going to inspire revival and social change... at least, it hasn't so far. Indeed, the last fifty years has been a golden age for End Times books and videos, so if anything, we should have seen an improvement in the spiritual condition—that is, if there were enduring value to those books. Their pessimism self-indicts.

The General Problem with Doomsday-ism

Pessimism about the future is not the sole province of religion. Secular Henny Pennys join in the church chorus of "The Sky is Falling," and sometimes scientists are guilty, too. Some scientists do not have enough faith in God, and some do not have enough faith in the resiliency of Planet Earth's ecosystem. In the Seventies, enough scientists feared a coming Ice Age that TIME magazine featured a cover story warning that by 2010, global cooling would be a significant worry. At least one End Time propheteer recently latched onto this old fear of "global dimming," which is a real consequence of air pollution blocking sunlight. In his fearmongering book of prophecy, *Final Warning*, Carl

Gallups called it a fulfillment of the Book of Revelation's warning that one-third of the light from the sun, moon and stars would be dimmed. But global dimming has never come close to blocking 33% of sunlight, and global warming has counterbalanced any significant cooling effect of global dimming. In 2012, the American Meteorological Society concluded that, largely because of improved pollution standards, solar radiation changes observed since 2001 show "no globally coherent trends anymore."[39]

Whether it be the resiliency of life on our planet, or the triumph of love over evil, things have a way of working out, in the long run, for the good… something the New Testament tells us. This is not to say we should be cavalier in the realm of science with concerns about the earth's environment, nor should we be unconcerned about the workings of evil in the spiritual realm. In the example of problems with our atmosphere, early concerns prompted action. A good end-result came because of Clean Air laws passed by concerned governments over the last four decades. So a little fear can be okay if it prompts us to healthy caution and action. But a paralyzing, "all-is-lost," defeatist pessimism serves only the Devil. Scientists were also correct to warn us about the dangers of nuclear radiation, and the darkest pessimists almost succeeded in shutting down the nuclear power industry entirely. Now many environmentalists are coming to believe this was a mistake, because less nuclear has meant more coal-burning, which causes a worldwide problem of global warming. When the nuclear industry has used the proper plant designs, nuclear energy production has proven much safer than many of the alternatives. Of course, the notable failures of Three Mile Island and Fukushima are terrible exceptions, but we must keep our doomsdayism in perspective: more people were killed in forest fires than in these fluke incidents. Our fear of forest fires does not warrant us bulldozing down our forests!

In the same book just mentioned, *Final Warning*, Carl Callups (and I wonder how he could possibly write a *sequel* to something entitled FINAL) also churns up fears about nuclear radiation, citing the Chernobyl nuclear accident as fulfillment of a bitter poisoning called "Wormwood," prophesied in Revelation. Chernobyl is Russian for wormwood, it is claimed. But that is not true. "Chernobyl" is the name of a plant that is a cousin to wormwood, which in English is called mugwort. A Russian translator confused the two terms, starting the false rumor. But even if true, did the nuclear accident at Chernobyl kill one-third of all life on earth and sea, as Revelation's poison Wormwood is predicted to cause? Now 28 years have passed since the Chernobyl partial-meltdown, and so far, less than 60 people have died from the explosion and radiation. Most citizens moved back into the area years ago, and cancer rates due to radiation poisoning have not soared there. I don't wish to minimize the tragic loss of 60 Russians, but far more people die *every single day* in the U.S. in traffic accidents! Again, the pessimists have been proved wrong. Not a little bit wrong, but wrong at an exponential level!

Optimism for the Future Church

The preponderance of evidence suggests that humanity will be around for many more decades. That means our energies should be devoted to building up the Church of Jesus Christ (the universal church, not any single denomination). We should quit expending our thought, study and energy on things we can't control or predict, and instead focus on making the Church relevant to the younger generations.

Though many denominations are in decline, Christianity is growing in the Third World. In the U.S., there are signs that the newest generation is receptive to the Christian church—just not as it is currently structured. Young people have very little interest in doctrines and denominations; they become excited by being personally and physically involved in mission projects for the needy.

   The majority of youth in America live in fractured families (either with a single parent or with divorced, reshuffled and remarried parents). Depression and despair run high among our young. The last thing they need is the repeated admonition that the world is ending in a few weeks. The message that world war, destruction and tribulation is right around the corner is terribly discouraging to youth, especially a generation that seems (overall) to have an attitude of "We could make the world better." This attitude should be our guidepost as Christians—even if we *do* believe this world is temporary.

Disillusionment and Minutia

   The next batch of potential missionaries may have no church connection yet... mostly because the video-game generation finds church stultifyingly boring. Kids have been bored in church for a long, long time... that's not breaking news. Novelist Kent Haruf (author of the book, *Plainsong*) admits that when he was growing up, "I hated Sunday School, because nothing ever happened. We would *endure* church." And he was a preacher's son! My father was a minister, too, and none of his three sons have much enthusiasm for denominational churches. When even those of us who were raised and nurtured in Christianity still turn out to be disaffected adults, it spells trouble. Some are disaffected because the Institution of Church offered stale, outdated programming. Our audience has become accustomed to special effects, explosions and titillation in media, drawing a stark contrast to the wordy, monotonous sermons coming from all too many pulpits. In an age of polished, edited sound-bytes, church has way too many words and redundancies, whether it be in mainstream churches (too much lectionary) or contemporary churches (too much time spent on parish announcements, mindless repetitive choruses, and random chit-chat). Others become disillusioned because so much of conservative Christianity seems at odds with modern science and culture. Promised revivals and promised miracles and promised "end of days" that never come true feed a feeling of cynicism. Others lose zeal when they see double-standards among religious leaders: from the sexual antics and hypocrisy of those like Jim Bakker, Jimmy Swaggart, and Terry Smith, to the many ministers who forget about Jesus' compassion for the poor, who treasure too much gold and live in sumptuous mansions.[40] I must ask God to forgive my critical spirit, and of course my own hypocrisy in that I was not a perfect pastor... but surely, can't we do better?

If the Ship is Sinking, Change Chairs

At issue here is a proper prioritization of time and focus. As the cliché goes, *Why are we re-arranging the deck chairs on the Titanic?* The entire End Times topic is a side-show distraction to what Christianity should be focused upon, but **even within/among End Times speculations, we find endless sub-topic arguments**: "Do you believe in a pre-Trib, mid-Trib, or post-Trib rapture? Will the antichrist be European or Islamic or American? Are you a millennialist, an amillennialist, or a post-millennialist?"

What is it about religion that prompts people to debate minutia? In the 17th-century, William Chillingworth reported that unnamed scholastics had debated, "Whether a Million of Angels may not fit upon a needle's point?" Even the wise Thomas Aquinas had pondered if "several angels," being ethereal, could "be in the same place" simultaneously.

Two co-workers from different denominations were talking about their different perspectives on faith, and one explained that even within his denomination, there had been a split over a minor point of doctrine: "One group believes in a pre-Tribulation rapture, and the other in a post-Tribulation rapture," he explained. "There have been heated arguments and strife over the issue for as long as anyone can remember. But I feel sure my group has chosen the right side on this issue." Whereupon his friend inquired, "Which does your group believe in: the pre-Trib or the post-Trib?" And the first man paused, then replied, "For the life of me, I can't remember."

In retrospect, History so far has made the propheteers, the End Times exploiters, look like the punchline of a joke. So far, they haven't gotten much of anything right, and if it weren't for the cash incentive, I can't imagine why they'd bother to keep trying. The irony may be that when Christian leaders finally give up on their arrogant guessing game, maybe then Jesus *will* return!

Conclusion: The Thing Most Needful

To the reader's surprise, let me close by **embracing two quotes *from* the authors I've criticized**, quotes with which I **wholeheartedly agree**... the first, from Jeffrey Cahn:

"Every heartbeat is borrowed. Everything in this world that draws us or repels us, entangles us or compels us, everything we seek after, dwell on, or live for, is temporary, fleeting, and passing away. Therefore the meaning of this life is not found in anything of this life, but only in Him who lies behind it. And the purpose of this life is not found in seeking anything of this life, but only in seeking Him who gave it." That is a wonderfully true message... but it does not require the threat of Armageddon to drive it home. Even if the world doesn't end in this millennium, individual lives can be short, so those words should move us regardless.

And from Perry Stone's End Times book, I find another point of agreement. I quote it here in closing:

"If you don't know [Jesus] as you should… ask Christ to come into your life and change you so that your name will be inscribed in the most important book there is—the Lamb's Book of Life!"

If you trust in Jesus Christ, you need not fear whatever the future holds for you, whether that be Tribulation and Rapture years from now, or a car wreck or coronary tomorrow. As Jesus said in John 14: "Do not let your hearts be troubled. You believe in God; believe also in me.... I go and prepare a place for you, I will come back and take you to be with me...."

So in the end, it is not about me making preparations for the end of the world, it is about the preparations God has already made *for* us in the life beyond.

Maranatha!

~~~

The End?

ENDNOTES:

1. George R. Knight, *Millennial Fever and the End of the World*, (Boise, Idaho, Pacific Press, 1993), p. 218.
2. www.biography.com/people/tim-lahaye-204548 or www.catholic.com/documents/false-profit-money-prejudice-and-bad-theology-in-tim-lahaye%E2%80%99s-left-behind-series
3. Jonathan Cahn, *The Mystery of the Shemitah: The 3,000-Year-Old Mystery That Holds the Secret of America's Future, the World's Future, and Your Future!* (Frontline: 2014)
4. www.watchfortheday.org/tetrad20142015.html
5. quoted in *The Washington Post*, April 3rd, 2015
6. Cahn, *The Mystery of the Shemitah*
7. www.endtime.com/pdf/archives/ETM-2007-09-Two-Billion.pdf
8. www.endtime.com/world-war-three/
9. Tax Policy Center Table T13-0020
10. Cahn, The Mystery of the Shemitah
11. ibid
12. www.imf.org/external/np/seminars/eng/2012/fincrises/pdf/ch8.pdf
13. www.en.wikipedia.org/wiki/List_of_dates_predicted_for_apocalyptic_events#cite_ref-shaw_41-5
14. Hal Lindsey, *The Late Great Planet Earth*, (1970, Zondervan, Grand Rapids, MI), pp. 145-146
15. ibid, p. 54
16. Eva Shaw, *Eve of Destruction*, (Lowell House, Los Angeles, 1995)
17. CBN broadcast, June 9, 1982
18. www.religioustolerance.org/end_wrl2.htm
19. www.rightwingwatch.org/content/bible-code-definitively-proves-obama-antichrist#sthash.pqTOGn5m.dpuf
20. Tacitus, *Annals, Volume XV*
21. www.washingtonpost.com/wp-dyn/content/article/2007/01/24/AR2007012400371_pf.html
22. www.urbanlegends.about.com/library/bl-obama-wedding-ring.htm
23. www.rickross.com/reference/tv_preachers/tv_preachers7.html and www.inplainsite.org/html/tele-evangelist_lifestyles.html
24. www.inplainsite.org/html/tele-evangelist_lifestyles.html
25. www.cbsdallas.files.wordpress.com/2011/01/emic-copeland-01-5-11.pdf
26. *The Atlantic*, March 2015

27. www.mysanantonio.com/news/local/article/Hagee-America-has-rewarded-laziness-and-we-ve-5674351.php
28. *The Interpreter's Dictionary of the Bible*, (Abingdon Press, 1962,) p. 437, *Magog*
29. Merrill Unger, *Beyond The Crystal Ball*, p. 81.
30. Joel Richardson, *The Islamic Antichrist: The Shocking Truth about the Real Nature of the Beast*
31. www.globalfirepower.com/countries-comparison.asp
32. www.brookings.edu/projects/archive/nucweapons/50.aspx
33. Cahn, *The Mystery of the Shemitah*
34. using 2011 data; www://taxfoundation.org/article/summary-latest-federal-income-tax-data
35. cited in *The Washington Post*, "The Fix" column, November 14, 2014
36. cited in *Mother Jones.com* magazine, Feb. 3, 2012
37. www.leftcall.com/4557/u-s-crime-rates-1960-2010-the-facts-might-surprise-you
38. *Time* magazine, July 3, 2013
39. July 8, 2011 *Journal of the American Meteorological Society*
40. www.pmiministries.com/Liars_Hypocrites_Deceivers.htm

•All Bible quotes are from the NIV translation, ©1984 Zondervan, unless noted otherwise in the text.
•Yet another disclaimer: this book does not contain an enormous amount of cited references (except for Scripture quotes, which are many, but are cited within the text). And the endnotes do not all contain page numbers. There are four reasons for this:
1. This is not intended to be a textbook or academic study. It is aimed at general readers. I do thank Carey Moore, Professor of Math, Physics and Astronomy at the University of West Alabama, for his input and review.
2. The amount of internet resources, beginning with "Google," are so vast that it is now a very easy thing to search and find verification for all the facts I offer herein.
3. When reading source books, I often used Kindle ebooks, which lack fixed page numbers.
4. I lack the funds for a research department. Other than my editor, I have no staff. Your pardon is requested.
    ~the author

OTHER BOOKS BY LANCE MOORE:

NON-FICTION
•**Killing JFK: 50 Years, 50 Lies**
From the Warren Commission to Bill O'Reilly, a History of Deceit in the Kennedy Assassination

•**Class Crucifixion: Money, Power, Religion and the Death of the Middle Class:** An examination of the ethics of class structure, wealth inequality, and greed.

•**Firm Foundations: An Architect and a Pastor Guide Your Church Construction**: A practical guide for church building committee members and pastors.

INSPIRATIONAL:
•**The Neurotic's Guide to God and Love: Seven Mistakes that Make Us Crazy, and Eight Ways to Change:** Moving in faith from guilt and shame toward a life rooted in love and grace.

•**Outdoors with God: Finding God in the Great Outdoors**: A devotional book of essays about God's grandeur, beauty and power as displayed in Creation.

FICTION:
•**Majestic Twelve... Minus One**
A riveting tale spun from true government documents about the mysterious "Operation Majestic 12."

To order direct from the publisher, or for more information, please go to:

www.Sky-Fy.com

Most titles are also on ebook via Amazon Kindle.

Printed in Great Britain
by Amazon.co.uk, Ltd.,
Marston Gate.